ESSAYS IN
GREEK PHILOSOPHY

ESSAYS IN
GREEK PHILOSOPHY

BY

RICHARD ROBINSON

FELLOW OF ORIEL COLLEGE
OXFORD

CLARENDON PRESS · OXFORD

1969

Oxford University Press, Ely House, London W.1

GLASGOW NEW YORK TORONTO MELBOURNE WELLINGTON
CAPE TOWN SALISBURY IBADAN NAIROBI LUSAKA ADDIS ABABA
BOMBAY CALCUTTA MADRAS KARACHI LAHORE DACCA
KUALA LUMPUR SINGAPORE HONG KONG TOKYO

PRINTED IN GREAT BRITAIN
BY THE CAMELOT PRESS LTD.,
LONDON AND SOUTHAMPTON

This collection consists of seven papers in ancient philosophy, originally published in various journals at various dates from 1936 to 1956, and now reprinted as a book. The first of these papers, 'Analysis in Greek Geometry', is primarily about Greek mathematicians; but it bears on the interpretation of Plato's Divided Line. The next five essays are directly about Plato. All of these essays are reprinted very nearly as originally published. But the seventh and last essay, which concerns Aristotle's doctrine of incontinence, was first written and published in French, and is here presented in an English translation.

R. R.

CONTENTS

ANALYSIS IN GREEK GEOMETRY

(First printed in Mind *in 1936)*

THE historians of Greek mathematics are at one about the method that the Greek geometers called analysis.[1] Professor Cornford, however, has recently rejected their account and offered a new one.[2] In this note I shall first give the usual view of analysis, then give Professor Cornford's view, and lastly argue that Professor Cornford is mistaken and the usual view correct.

The accepted version of analysis is as follows. It was a method of discovery, a method of discovering either the proofs of geometrical propositions or the solutions of geometrical problems. It was followed by a synthesis, and the latter constituted in the first place a check on the analysis, to make sure that there had been no error; but, secondly, provided that there had been no error, it constituted the actual proof or solution for the sake of which the analysis was undertaken. I give here a simple schematic illustration of analysis and synthesis applied to the proof of a proposition.

Suppose I want to prove, if possible, the proposition (1). Then, if I am to work by the method of analysis, I proceed as follows. First I assume that (1) is true; assume, that is, what I really want to prove. Then I consider what follows from (1).

---

[1] I have verified this statement for Hankel (*Zur Geschichte der Mathematik in Alterthum und Mittelalter* (1874), pp. 137–49), Cantor (*Geschichte der Mathematik*, 2nd ed., i, 207 ff.) and Heath (*The Thirteen Books of Euclid's Elements*, i, 137 ff.). None of these three authors mentions any dissenting view about what the method was. The following view account of analysis is based on their statements.

[2] In the course of an article on 'Mathematics and Dialectic in the *Republic*, VI–VII', *Mind*, N.S., xli, 43–7.

Say I find that (1) implies (2). Then I consider what follows from (2). Say I find that (2) implies (3). I go on in this way until I reach a proposition that I already know to be true. Say (5) is such a proposition. It does not matter *how* (5) is known, provided only that it *is* known and known independently of (1). It may be an axiom, or a theorem previously demonstrated, or an element of the construction. When such a proposition is reached the analysis is over and the synthesis may begin. The synthesis consists in going through the same steps in the reverse order: 'Since (5) is known to be true, therefore (4) is true and therefore (3) is true and therefore (2) is true and therefore (1) is true, which was to be proved.'

For this method to work, the implications must be reciprocal. Not merely must (1) imply (2), but (2) must imply (1). The chain 1–2–3–4–5 must give an unbroken series of necessitations whichever way you proceed along it. In other words, the propositions concerned must be convertible. Convertibility is easy to obtain in mathematics, which consists largely of propositions asserting symmetrical relations (such as equations) and therefore convertible. But if in your analysis you should use any inconvertible propositions, you will discover that you have done so when you try to make your synthesis. You may discover, for example, that (2) does not entail (1) although (1) entails (2). This is the way in which the synthesis tests the analysis. If, on the other hand, the chain 5–4–3–2–1, when taken in this order, makes a necessary inference, your synthesis constitutes the proof that you were seeking; for (5) is independently known to be true, and (5) mediately entails (1), and (1) is what was to be proved.[1]

---

[1] The point that you may be unable to complete your synthesis, and that this is a sign that the analysis was unsuccessful, is not clearly made in any ancient text known to me. In making this point the historians of mathematics are apparently not repeating what the Greeks actually said, but telling us what is involved in what the Greeks said and did. However,

If proposition (5), the last proposition in the analysis, were independently known to be false instead of being independently known to be true, the analysis would have shown us that (1) was false (since true premisses cannot validly lead to a false conclusion), and therefore that our attempt to find a proof of (1) could not succeed, and it would have shown us this without the aid of any synthesis. Thus we may widen our account of analysis and say that it is a method for either discovering the proof of a given proposition or discovering that that proposition cannot be proved because it is false.

The *reductio ad absurdum* is a special case of the method of analysis. If (5) is false, (1) is false; and if (1) is false, the contradictory of (1) is true. We can therefore prove the contradictory of (1) by assuming (1) and showing that it entails (5), which is an absurdity and as such independently known to be false.

The application of the method of analysis to the solution of problems is similar. You assume the problem solved and infer consequences from that assumption until you reach a consequence that you are able to construct. Then you make that construction and proceed backwards to what is required.

Such is the usual view of analysis. I will quote here Heath's translation of a part of Pappus which is one of the main passages on which it is based.

Analysis then takes that which is sought as if it were admitted and passes from it through its successive consequences ($\delta\iota\grave{\alpha}\ \tau\hat{\omega}\nu$ $\dot{\epsilon}\xi\hat{\eta}s\ \dot{\alpha}\kappa o\lambda o\acute{\upsilon}\theta\omega\nu$) to something which is admitted as the result of synthesis: for in analysis we assume that which is sought as if it were (already) done ($\gamma\epsilon\gamma o\nu\acute{o}s$), and we inquire what it is from which this results, and again what is the antecedent cause of

I have noticed two passages that may possibly be references to this point. 'Therefore D × AC is either greater than BE² × EA or equal to it or less than it. If it is greater, there will be no synthesis, as has been shown in the analysis' (Eutocius, see Archimedes (ed. Heiberg), iii, 160, 10). The other passage is Aristotle, *Soph. El.*, 16, 175a 28: 'In diagrams we can sometimes analyse the figure, but not construct it again.'

the latter, and so on, until by so retracing our steps we come upon something already known or belonging to the class of first principles, and such a method we call analysis as being solution backwards (ἀνάπαλιν λύσιν).

But in synthesis, reversing the process, we take as already done that which was last arrived at in the analysis and, by arranging in their natural order as consequences what were before antecedents, and successively connecting them one with another, we arrive finally at the construction of what was sought; and this we call synthesis.

Now analysis is of two kinds, the one directed to searching for the truth and called *theoretical*, the other directed to finding what we are told to find and called *problematical*. (1) In the *theoretical* kind we assume what is sought as if it were existent and true, after which we pass through its successive consequences (τῶν ἑξῆς ἀκολούθων), as if they too were true and established by virtue of our hypothesis, to something admitted: then (*a*), if that something admitted is true, that which is sought will also be true and the proof will correspond in the reverse order to the analysis, but (*b*), if we come upon something admittedly false, that which is sought will also be false. (2) In the *problematical* kind we assume that which is propounded as if it were known, after which we pass through its successive consequences (τῶν ἑξῆς ἀκολούθων), taking them as true, up to something admitted: if then (*a*) what is admitted is possible and obtainable, that is, what mathematicians call *given*, what was originally proposed will also be possible, and the proof will again correspond in reverse order to the analysis, but if (*b*) we come upon something admittedly impossible, the problem will also be impossible.[1]

And here is the same translator's version of a description of analysis and synthesis which, though not by Euclid, is found in the manuscripts of Euclid's *Elements*, XIII.

Analysis is an assumption of that which is sought as if it were admitted [and the passage] through its consequences (διὰ τῶν ἀκολούθων) to something admitted (to be) true. Synthesis is an

[1] Heath, op. cit., i, 138. In Hultsch's edition the text appears on pp. 634–6.

assumption of that which is admitted [and the passage] through its consequences (διὰ τῶν ἀκολούθων) to the finishing or attainment of what is sought.[1]

So far as I know, there are no other surviving ancient descriptions of analysis nearly as informative as that of Pappus. All the others either take still more knowledge for granted in the reader, or are unintelligible, or may refer to some non-geometrical kind of analysis.[2]

I turn now to the second part of my note, the statement of Professor Cornford's view of analysis. The following is, I hope, a fair and full statement of his view.

The method of analysis does not begin by asking what 1 implies, as the historians assert. It begins by asking *what would imply 1*. If I find that 2 would imply 1, I ask myself whether I know that 2 is true. If I do know this the analysis is over; but if not, I must go on to a second step. And, as before, this second step will not be asking what 2 implies but what

[1] Op. cit., i, 138. For the Greek see Euclid (ed. Heiberg), iv, 364–6.
[2] There are eight other passages known to me. (1) The passage in Euclid already quoted. (2) Proclus, *Euclid* (ed. Friedlein), 211, 12 ff. (3) Op. cit., 255, 8 ff. (4) Ammonius, *Comm. in Aristotelis Anal. Prior.* (ed. Wallies), 5, 5 ff., esp. 5, 26 ff. This gives Geminus' account of geometrical analysis and compares it with five other kinds of analysis, in the course of an attempt to answer the question why Aristotle called his book *Analytics*. (5) Anaritius, *Euclid* (ed. Curtze), 89. This gives a Latin translation of Al-Nairizi's Arabic translation of some observations by Hero which may have been about geometrical analysis, but in the course of the two translations Hero's meaning seems to have become unascertainable. (6) Themistius, *Arist. Anal. Post* (ed. Wallies), 26, 23. Professor Cornford thinks this refers to geometrical analysis (see his article, p. 45). (7) Aristotle, *EN*, iii, 3, 1112b20 ff. Professor Cornford thinks this too refers to geometrical analysis (ibid., 44). (8) Aristotle, *An. Post*, i, 23. Solmsen apparently thinks that this gives an account of the same kind of analysis as was used in geometry (*Die Entwicklung der aristotelischen Logik und Rhetorik*, pp. 121–4). He probably refers especially to 84b31–85a1. It seems to be the current view that Aristotle uses the word *analysis* in only one sense, and that the sense in question is the geometrical (cf. Einarson, *AJP*, January 1936). But I am not yet convinced even of the doctrine that Aristotle always uses the word in the same sense. The doctrine seems to be descended from Waitz' statement in his commentary, i, 366.

would imply 2. The process will continue until I come to something I do know. Let this be 5. Then I have finished the analysis and can make my synthesis: '5 is true, and 5 implies 4 implies 3 implies 2 implies 1, and 1 is what was to be proved.'

On this account analysis is not a process of deduction. I do not deduce 2 from 1. Only when I proceed in the reverse direction and make a synthesis am I performing an inference. In the analysis the activity of my mind is not demonstration but *intuition*. The analysing geometer *divines* the premiss (2) from which the conclusion (1) follows. Proclus was right when he described analysis in terms reminiscent of the upward path of dialectic in Plato's Divided Line, for that upward path is a series of intuitions.[1] 'It is certain that in his account of the dialectical ascent Plato is describing the upward movement of thought which has been illustrated from geometrical analysis.'[2]

On this account the implications with which analysis deals would not necessarily be reciprocal. There might be no entailment whatever in the direction from 1 to 5. Analysis would be going the wrong way along a one-way street, and synthesis would be coming back in the right direction.

In accordance with this view Professor Cornford criticizes the usual interpretation of the Pappus-passage as follows:

I gather from Sir T. Heath's discussion of this passage (*Thirteen Books of Euclid*, i, 138) that modern historians of mathematics— 'careful studies' by Hankel, Duhamel, and Zeuthen, and others by Ofterdinger and Cantor are cited—have made nonsense of much of it by misunderstanding the phrase '*the succession of sequent steps*' (τῶν ἑξῆς ἀκολούθων) as meaning logical 'consequences', as if it were τὰ συμβαίνοντα. Some may have been misled by Gerhardt (Pappus, vii, viii, Halle, 1871), who renders it '*Folgerungen*'. They have then been at great pains to show how the premises of a

---

[1] Proclus, *Euclid* (ed. Friedlein), 211, 20.
[2] *Mind*, N.S., xli, 47.

demonstration can be the consequences of the conclusion. The whole is clear when we see—what Pappus says—that the same sequence of steps is followed in both processes—*upwards* in Analysis, from the consequence to premisses implied in that consequence, and *downwards* in Synthesis, when the steps are reversed to frame the theorem or demonstrate the construction 'in the natural (logical) order'. You cannot follow the same series of steps first one way, then the opposite way, and arrive at logical *consequences* in both directions. And Pappus never said you could. He added ἑξῆς to indicate that the steps 'follow in *succession*' but are not, as ἀκόλουθα alone would suggest, logically 'consequent' in the upward direction. In the definitions of Analysis and Synthesis interpolated in Euclid XIII . . . the phrase διὰ τῶν ἀκολούθων is used in the same way: 'Analysis is a taking of the thing sought as admitted (and the passage) *through the sequent steps* to some admitted truth'. Here again it is translated by Heiberg (Teubner edit., III, 365) '*per consequentias*', and by Heath 'through its consequences'. These definitions may have been copied, with abbreviation, from Pappus' statement.[1]

Professor Cornford accordingly renders διὰ τῶν ἑξῆς ἀκολούθων as 'through the sequent steps' each of the three times that it occurs in Pappus. His view is that Pappus means a succession that is merely temporal, not also logical. In the synthesis the succession of steps is logical as well as temporal, but in the analysis it is not; for, whereas the synthesis is deduction, the analysis is intuition.

This completes the second part of my note, which was the presentation of Professor Cornford's view of analysis. In the third and last part, which is the attempt to show that Professor Cornford is wrong and the traditional view is right, I shall urge three points: first that he is influenced by a doubtful *a priori* principle, second that he cannot account for a vitally important set of texts, and third that his interpretation of Pappus is mistaken.

[1] Op. cit., p. 47, n. 1. The reference to Heiberg's ed. of Euclid should be iv, 365.

First, then, I venture to suggest that Professor Cornford is under the influence of a doubtful *a priori* principle. He has stated the principle himself: 'You cannot follow the same series of steps first one way, then the opposite way, and arrive at logical *consequences* in both directions' (p. 47, n.). If this principle were true, the method of analysis as described by the historians of mathematics would be *a logical impossibility*; and if the Greek geometers really thought they used such a method, they were grossly mistaken either in their geometry or in their methodology. Professor Cornford is naturally loath to suppose that the great Greek geometers habitually practised a logical absurdity. And if the historians of mathematics also thought it a logical absurdity they would undoubtedly reconsider their ascription of it to the founders of geometry, and try to reinterpret the texts. I cannot help feeling that Professor Cornford's whole attempt to reinterpret Pappus is due simply to his *a priori* conviction that the meaning commonly attributed to that passage is absurd.

But is it a logical absurdity? In these days when logic is making such surprising developments and so greatly inincreasing its powers, we may, I think, legitimately marvel at Professor Cornford's flat statement that the same series of steps will not give logical consequences in either direction, especially when his own university has been so prominent in these new developments. The following three propositions seem to form a series that will give logical consequences in either direction: (1) $3x = 4y$, (2) $3x + y = 5y$, (3) $3x + 2y = 6y$. And when I gave the conventional account of Greek analysis to a mathematical friend he replied that, while he did not see why they called it 'analysis', he himself practised it every day!

That Professor Cornford's *a priori* principle is doubtful will become much more evident if we turn to our second argument against him, namely that he fails to explain a vitally important set of texts. The fact is that there are two entirely different kinds of text that may be consulted to discover what the Greek geometers meant by analysis. The first is the text that gives a theoretical description of analysis, the text that belongs more properly to logic or methodology than to geometry. In Professor Cornford's article, and in this note down to the present sentence, only the first kind of text has been discussed. But the Greeks have not left us merely descriptions of their analysis; they have left us also *examples*! And whereas their surviving descriptions are few and meagre, their surviving examples are copious and clear. There are numerous geometrical propositions attacked by the method of analysis in Archimedes' second book *On the Sphere and Cylinder*. There are many such in Pappus himself. Surely we ought to base ourselves on these actual examples rather than on the descriptions. That, at any rate, is how the historians of mathematics formulated their unanimous view.[1]

I will translate here a very simple example. I believe it will show clearly, first, that the writer thought he was doing what Professor Cornford says is impossible, and, second, that in a certain reasonable sense he really was doing that. The definitions of analysis and synthesis found in the manuscripts of Euclid, which we have already mentioned, are followed by proofs of Euclid, XIII, 1–5, by this method, and I choose the proof of XIII, 1, which says that 'if a straight line be cut in extreme and mean ratio, the square on the greater segment added to the half of the whole is five times the square on the half.'[2]

---

[1] Hankel's illustration of analysis is actually taken from Pappus, cf. his *Geschichte der Mathematik*, p. 143, and Pappus 830, Hultsch. For the analytical proofs of Euclid, XIII, 2–5 see Euclid (ed. Heiberg), IV, 368 ff. For Archimedes see Archimedes (ed. Heiberg), i, 191 ff., or Heath's translation.

[2] Euclid (ed. Heiberg), iv, 366, 3 ff. This is not the regular proof of xiii, 1, and is not by Euclid himself, for he does not use analysis. My version is based on Heiberg's Latin translation, loc. cit.

The Analysis and the Synthesis of Prop. 1 without a figure

For let the straight line AB be cut in extreme and mean ratio at C, and let the greater segment be AC, and let $AD = \frac{1}{2}AB$.

I say that $CD^2 = 5AD^2$.

For, since

(1) ... $CD^2 = 5AD^2$

and

(i) ... $CD^2 = CA^2 + AD^2 + 2CA \times AD$ [II, 4].

therefore

(2) ... $CA^2 + AD^2 + 2CA \times AD = 5AD^2$.

Therefore, by subtraction,

(3) ... $CA^2 + 2CA \times AD = 4AD^2$.

But (since $BA = 2AD$)

(ii) ... $BA \times AC = 2CA \times AD$.

And (since AB has been cut in extreme and mean ratio)

(iii) ... $AC^2 = AB \times BC$.

Therefore

(4) ... $BA \times AC + AB \times BC = 4AD^2$.

But

(iv) ... $BA \times AC + AB \times BC = AB^2$ [II, 2].

Therefore

(5) ... $AB^2 = 4AD^2$

and this is true, for $AB = 2AD$ [by construction].

Synthesis

Now since

(5) ... $AB^2 = 4AD^2$

and

(iv) ... $BA^2 = BA \times AC + AB \times BC$ [II, 2],

therefore

(4) ... $BA \times AC + AB \times BC = 4AD^2$.

But

(ii) ... $BA \times AC = 2DA \times AC$

and

(iii) . . . $AB \times BC = AC^2$.
  Therefore
(3) . . . $AC^2 + 2DA \times AC = 4DA^2$,
  and therefore
(2) . . . $DA^2 + AC^2 + 2DA \times AC = 5DA^2$.
  But
(i) . . . $DA^2 + AC^2 + 2DA \times AC = CD^2$ [II, 4].
  Therefore
(1) . . . $CD^2 = 5DA^2$,
  which was to be proved.

Analysis.

$$1 \to 2 \to 3 \to 4 \to 5$$
$$\uparrow \quad \nearrow \nwarrow \uparrow$$
$$\text{i} \quad \text{ii} \quad \text{iii iv}$$

Synthesis.

$$5 \to 4 \to 3 \to 2 \to 1$$
$$\uparrow \nearrow \nwarrow \quad \uparrow$$
$$\text{iv ii iii} \quad \text{i}$$

The accompanying diagrams show the nature of the reasoning. In the analysis the implication goes from 1 by way of 2 and 3 and 4 to 5. In the synthesis it goes from 5 by way of 4 and 3 and 2 to 1, which is precisely the reverse. The propositions identified with Roman numerals are necessary to connect the other propositions together; they are not, however, links in the chain but merely pins that hold the links together. Here then there really seems to be a two-way street of inference.

It might be objected that the example is not really a two-way street of inference precisely because of the presence of the propositions with Roman numerals. The so called inference from 1 to 2 is really an inference from 1 + i to 2; and therefore it is not the reverse of the so called inference from 2 to 1, for the latter is really the inference from 2 + i to 1.

To this objection two things may be said. In the first place, we all think in enthymemes; that is, we regard A as following from B when it really follows from B + C. Even when we are conscious of the necessity for C, as in the above geometrical example, we often regard A as following from B rather than from B + C; and the reason for this is sometimes that C is an old and standing element of our thought, a presupposition under which all our thinking proceeds, while A and B are new elements; they are the actual present process of our thinking. Thus in the above example anything previously proved in Euclid II functions here not as a stage in the present demonstration but as a condition controlling the course of it. The construction functions in the same way.

If our tendency to regard some of our premisses as being the banks of the stream of thought and not any part of the water—if this tendency involves an erroneous view of thinking, then the above example is not really a series of identical steps taken first one way and then the other, and the author was mistaken in supposing that it was, and all the Greek geometers were mistaken in so far as their analyses and syntheses demanded adventitious premisses lying outside the series itself. Along this line of thought, therefore, we answer the objection by more or less admitting it, by admitting, that is, that in a really strict use of language the synthesis does not traverse exactly the same steps as the analysis.

The second answer consists in pointing to one particular step in our example, namely that from 2 to 3. Here there is no adventitious proposition, and therefore apparently the inference in the synthesis from 3 to 2 is the precise reverse. However, it might be maintained that even here there is a suppressed major premiss, the presence of which will make the synthesis different from the analysis. Whether this must always be true in the last resort is a difficult question of logic to which I do not know the answer; but I believe I have pursued the matter far enough to show two things: first, that in an ultimate and strict use of language Professor Cornford's *a priori* principle may be true; and, second, that in ordinary language there is a very natural and reasonable sense in which his principle is false. This conclusion is sufficient to vindicate the historians of mathematics from the charge of making 'nonsense' of Pappus. It remains to see whether they have 'lamentably misunderstood' him;[1] and that brings us to our third and last point, the argument that Professor Cornford's interpretation of Pappus is mistaken.

We have established the conclusions (1) that you *can*, in ordinary language, 'follow the same series of steps first one way, then the opposite way, and arrive at logical *consequences* in both directions'; and (2) that the Greek geometers frequently did so, and called the procedure analysis and synthesis. Hence there is no longer any objection to finding this meaning in Pappus, if it seems to be what he says. Now surely it does seem to be what he says. Τῶν ἑξῆς ἀκολούθων is more likely to mean a succession of logical consequences than a succession of sequent steps that are not logical consequences. Surely Professor Cornford has preferred the latter meaning only because he thinks that the former gives a logical monstrosity.

Professor Cornford leans heavily on the word ἑξῆς to support his interpretation of ἀκολούθων. Pappus 'added ἑξῆς to indicate that the steps "follow in succession" but are not, as ἀκόλουθα alone would suggest, logically "consequent" in the upward direction'. Yet in the Euclid-passage he is obliged to give the same sense to ἀκολούθων although there is no ἑξῆς; and hence he is obliged to suggest that the Euclid-passage was copied from Pappus, 'with abbreviation'. According to the historians, however, the Euclid-passage goes back to Eudoxus or at least to Hero, both of whom lived before Pappus.[2]

Professor Cornford has overlooked the fact that on his interpretation Pappus makes a mistake in logic. Pappus says that when, in theoretical analysis, we reach a ὁμολογούμενον or something admitted (sc. admitted to be true or admitted to

---

[1] Op. cit., p. 46.
[2] The theories are summarized in Heath's *Euclid*, I, 137.

be false), then, if it is admittedly false, the conclusion sought will be false also. This does not follow, on Professor Cornford's interpretation; for if in the chain 1–2–3–4–5 the implication holds only from 5 to 1, and not also from 1 to 5, then it is possible for 5 to be false and 1 to be nevertheless true, since false premisses can give rise to true conclusions. Pappus makes a corresponding statement about problematical analysis a few lines lower, and therefore, on Professor Cornford's interpretation, he makes the same mistake again. On the ordinary interpretation of analysis, however, since 1–2–3–4–5 is a chain of necessary implications whichever way you take it, Pappus is correct in saying that the falsity of 5 involves the falsity of 1.

There are two phrases in the Pappus-passage that at first sight favour Professor Cornford's interpretation, and I will conclude by examining them. 'In analysis we assume that which is sought . . . and inquire what it is from which this results, and again what is the antecedent cause of the latter, and so on, until by so retracing our steps we come upon something already known.' On the conventional view of analysis we might have expected him to say 'what results from this' instead of 'what it is from which this results'; and if this sentence were our only evidence about analysis Professor Cornford's account of that method would be preferable. On the other hand, this sentence is not incorrect on the usual view of analysis; it is merely unexpected. Since on the usual view the implication goes both ways Pappus would be correct whichever way he said it went. And his own phrase τῶν ἑξῆς ἀκολούθων, and above all the examples, show what the truth is. The reason why he expresses himself here in this unexpected way is that he is looking at analysis as existing for the sake of synthesis; this makes him describe the steps of the analysis, not as they appear while you are doing the analysis, but as they appear in the subsequent synthesis.

The other thing which at first sight favours Professor

Cornford's interpretation is the statement that synthesis takes the steps in their 'natural order'. But this can be given a good sense on the accepted view of analysis. The order in which propositions are taken in analysis is 'unnatural', in spite of the fact that it gives a necessary connection, because you start with a proposition that you do not know to be true and treat it as if you did know it to be true. This unnaturalness is very clear, in the example that we have studied, at the beginning of the analysis. The proposition that is set out in one line as to be proved is stated in the very next line as if it were already known.

I urge that these considerations sustain the historians' interpretation of the Pappus-passage against that of Professor Cornford.

2

PLATO'S CONSCIOUSNESS OF FALLACY

(First printed in Mind *in 1942)*

WHEN we read an argument in Plato's dialogues, our first impression is often that it is absurdly fallacious. Especially is this so in the early dialogues. The question therefore arises whether these arguments seemed as fallacious to Plato as they do to us, or whether he thought them valid. And this leads on to the further question what conception Plato had of fallacy as such? To what extent did he possess words for fallacy in general, or for special forms of it; to what extent had he a logical apparatus for dealing with it? This article (1) briefly surveys the types of fallacy in the early dialogues, and (2) attempts to answer the two questions thus raised.

Four sorts of fallacy are common in Plato's early dialogues: (1) fallacious question, (2) fallacious analogy, (3) fallacious conversion, and (4) ambiguity.

(1) A *question* is fallacious if it implies a falsehood. Every question implies a proposition. This is because a question expresses wonder, and wonder must be about something. It is impossible to wonder about nothing at all. In wondering we are therefore assuming the existence of some state of affairs, or the truth of some proposition. A question is fallacious, therefore, when the proposition which it implies is false.

Fallacious question in this sense is frequent in the dialogues. When, for example, Socrates asks what part of reality rhetoric concerns (*Go.* 449D), he is assuming, as the context shows, that there must be some part of reality that is dealt with by rhetoric and by no other science, if rhetoric is to be a science. The question of the *Lysis*, under what conditions friendship arises, assumes that there are universal and necessary conditions of friendship, and that they are very simple, perhaps so simple as to be expressed in a single word. Fallacious question is common in Plato's early dialogues in the form of offering an inexhaustive set of alternatives: 'Is A X or Y?', where the truth is that it is neither. Such a question can be made especially plausible by a fallacious use of the law of excluded middle. If Socrates asks us whether A is X or not-X we feel that it must be one or the other; and yet the question whether justice itself is just or unjust is probably fallacious (*Prot.* 330C; see Theodore de Laguna, *Philos. Review*, XLIII, 450 ff.). Socrates often succeeds in getting a universal proposition accepted by representing that the only alternative is the contrary ('Is A X or not-X?'), when the truth is that 'Some A is X and some is not' (e.g. *Go.* 507A7–9, *Alc.* I, 126C).

(2) The nature of fallacious *analogy* need not be elaborated here, nor need we emphasize its apparent frequency in Plato. On a first reading of the *Gorgias*, for example, we may think it wholly unfair to compare Pericles, whom the Athenians convicted of theft towards the end of his career, to a keeper whose animals should be worse tempered at the end of his charge than at the beginning (516A). Socrates' common analogy between virtue and art or τέχνη seems responsible for many fallacies.

(3) Fallacious *conversion* is assuming that all B is A when the premiss was only that all A is B. In the categorical syllogism it appears as the undistributed middle or as the illicit process. For if from all A's being B and all C's being B we infer that all C is A, it is because we have assumed that, since all A is B, all B is A; and if from all A's being B and no C's being A we infer that no C is B, it is again because we have assumed that, since all A is B, all B is A. In the hypothetical syllogism fallacious conversion is known as 'affirming

the consequent'. 'If X is A it is B; X is B; therefore X is A.' We have assumed that 'if X is A it is B' entails its converse 'if X is B it is A'. Examples of this fallacy in Plato will be better postponed to a later occasion.

(4) The nature of *ambiguity*, and its frequency in the dialogues, are sufficiently evident for our preliminary purpose. Every reader of the *Lysis* feels that the word φίλον there means sometimes lover and sometimes beloved, and that much of the argument turns on this equivocation. In the *Protagoras* (332) Socrates infers that wisdom and temperance are identical from these three premisses: (1) wisdom is opposite to *aphrosyne*; (2) temperance is opposite to *aphrosyne*; (3) nothing has more than one opposite. Here *aphrosyne* means folly in the first premiss but intemperance in the second.

In spite of the fallacious appearance of their arguments to us, Plato's characters often show a very high degree of confidence that their arguments are neither fallacious nor merely probable. 'Either we must abandon those doctrines or these conclusions must follow', says Socrates in the *Gorgias* (480E); and elsewhere in the same dialogue he refers to his arguments as 'iron and adamantine' (509A).

We come now to the first of our two questions: To what extent did Plato himself consider such arguments fallacious?

When the conclusion of an argument is false, this may be either because the inference is fallacious or because the premisses are false; and in philosophy it is hard to say which. In geometry perhaps we can always certainly distinguish between a false premiss and a fallacious inference; but the geometrical method has never worked in philosophy. The subject-matter is too fluid or too elastic, the distinction between axiom and theorem extremely hard to maintain. In philosophy, therefore, there is always danger of mistaking a false premiss for a fallacious inference; and that is what we are doing much of the time that we find fallacy in Plato.

There is a specially good reason why we should make this mistake with Plato, and that is that we often do not at first see what his premisses are. To take an example, the analogy between art and virtue shocks us only because we do not think what it really means. 'Art' is our translation of τέχνη, and τέχνη to Plato is identical with ἐπιστήμη or knowledge. 'Virtue' is our translation of ἀρετή, and ἀρετή to Plato and Socrates is essentially a form of knowledge. The premiss is, then, that ἀρετή and τέχνη are both knowledge; and there is no fallacy in treating them as analogous. Plato is merely saying that what is true of all forms of knowledge must be true of ἀρετή, since ἀρετή is a form of knowledge. What happens in this case is that because of the difficulty of thinking ourselves into Plato's strange world, and of remaining in it in spite of the pull of our modern conceptions, we fall back on the modern equivalents for his conceptions, and unfortunately they are not equivalent! And this is the explanation of many of the fallacies that we think we find.

Three of the four types of fallacy we have enumerated are perhaps more properly to be regarded as forms of falsity in the premisses. (1) Fallacious question is a way of obtaining a premiss. (2) All analogy is premiss before it is inference. (3) When we think we find fallacious conversion in Plato, the truth is often that he assumes the convertibility of the proposition as part of the premiss. Thus in *Republic*, I, 341C–342E, which looks like an illicit process of the minor term, Socrates is probably really premissing the equivalence of the minor and middle terms. He is taking for granted that all τέχνη is ἀρχή and all ἀρχή is τέχνη, which very likely seemed a probable premiss to him. Even in English, when we say that Aness is Bness, using abstract nouns without a sign of quantity, we think of the proposition as asserting an equivalence, and therefore convertible. Much more must this be so in Greek, whose far greater inflectedness makes word-order far less important, so that 'A is B' and 'B is A' tend to become identical when both are nouns, or at any rate when both are abstract nouns. A curious passage in the *Gorgias* (466A) seems to imply that in Greek if you say 'A is B' you will be understood to imply that B is A, and if you wish to avoid this implication you must say 'A is a sort of B' or 'A is a part of B'. The translation is this: 'What are you saying? Rhetoric seems to you to be flattery?—I said a part of flattery. Can you not remember at your age, Polus? What will you do next?' The same thing seems to be implied, though less distinctly, by this passage from the *Meno* (73E): 'Justice is virtue, Socrates.—Is it virtue, Meno, or *a* virtue?—How do do you mean?—Well, take anything you like. Take, say, roundness. I should say that roundness is *a* shape, not just simply shape. And the reason why I should say so is that there are other shapes.' Here Socrates seems to imply that if you say that justice is virtue you imply that virtue is justice.

In this way we can remove many of the apparently fallacious questions and analogies and conversions in the dialogues. They are not really fallacious, and therefore the question whether Plato was aware of their invalidity would itself be a fallacious question when applied to them. Nevertheless, there certainly remain in the dialogues many fallacies falling under each of these three heads; and in addition to all of them there is the great army of fallacies in the dialogues falling under the head of ambiguity, none of which can be explained away as falsehood in the premisses. The question is still legitimate, therefore, to what extent Plato was aware of the fallacies in his dialogues as fallacies.

The difficulty of this question is due to the nature of dialogue. The dialogue, being a form of drama, enables the author to set down opinions and arguments without expressing any judgement on their truth or validity. In fact, it makes it quite hard for him to indicate unmistakably what his judgement is. He may use a chorus or other recognized device to talk in his proper person; but Plato did not. To speak through the most prominent or the most sympathetic character is a much less certain means of communication; but it is the only one the dialogues employ. Its uncertainty has been well illustrated in the twentieth century by an enormous divergence of opinion on the question how far Plato does so speak. It thus comes about that for only a tiny fraction of the arguments he presents does Plato give us anything like a direct statement of his own view of their validity; and even in these cases the statement can only consist in a subsequent comment by one of the dramatis personae.

It is necessary to divide the dialogues into two groups, and answer the question separately for each group. All Platonic scholars hold that in the *Sophist* and subsequent works the protagonist expresses Plato's own views, except that Professor Taylor would exclude the *Timaeus* from this generalization. In the earliest dialogues, on the other hand, Plato's purpose is almost entirely to depict an unusual personality, and he has little or no interest in defending the logical validity of any argument which that person uses; he cares only to show that the argument, when it was used, effectually convicted of ignorance the man upon whom it was used. It remains perfectly possible that this conviction of ignorance took place through premisses that were in fact false, or through inferences that were in fact invalid. The earliest dialogues aim at depicting a person who aims, not at inculcating any positive truths, but at convicting men of ignorance in order to make them eager to seek virtue.

We can now answer the question separately for the two groups of dialogues that we have distinguished. In the latest dialogues, if the protagonist offers as a serious argument what is in fact a fallacy, then Plato himself failed to see the mistake. For example, if the explanation of the possibility of falsehood in the *Sophist* should seem to us a fallacy, we should be obliged to conclude that Plato here made a logical error.

In the earliest dialogues, on the other hand, there is no general reason for supposing that Plato was himself deceived by any fallacy by which he makes Socrates deceive another; and we ought to assume this, with regard to any particular fallacy, only if there is some special reason for doing so, as that this fallacy deceived all Athenians, or deceived Plato all his life. In the purely elenctic dialogues the fact that a fallacy passes for valid is not by itself any evidence that Plato thought it was so. Elenchus is essentially argument *ad hominem*. As the questioner has to find premisses that appeal to the answerer, so he has to find inferences that appeal to him; and, provided that he really does convince him, he may sometimes use premisses that he does not himself believe, and even inferences that he himself considers fallacious. Certainly Plato might put into Socrates' mouth an argument that Plato believed fallacious, but Socrates had actually used and used successfully. Probably he might think it a typical piece of Socratic mischief to bewilder a fool or stimulate a boy with a fallacious argument. Shorey is right, in principle at any rate, in saying that Plato was not himself deceived by the fallacy he set down in the *Lysis* (220E), but deliberately chose to make the appearance of bewilderment and the antithesis between the prime beloved and other beloveds as complete, as emphatic, and as symmetrical as possible (*Class. Phil.* XXV (1930), 380–3). When an early dialogue ends with a review of the argument in which Socrates takes a low opinion of its value, that is Plato's way of telling us that he knows the arguments are dubious. At the end of *Republic*, I, Socrates says they have got nothing out of the discussion because they have failed to persevere with any one question until it was answered. At the end of the *Charmides* he notes that they have committed many deliberate inconsistencies. At the end of the *Lysis* he emphasizes their helplessness in the search for the nature of friendship. At the end of the

Protagoras he declares the argument to have been a terrible topsy-turvy confusion (361C).

So much for the question to what extent Plato was aware of the fallacies in the arguments he attributed to his characters. We turn now to our other question: What consciousness had Plato of fallacy as such?

On general grounds we must believe that Plato, during at any rate a large part of his creative years, was aware in some way of the general nature and possibility of fallacy. When the greatness of a great man expresses itself frequently in highly formalized and explicit chains of deduction, it stands to reason that the possibility of fallacy must occur to him in some shape. And we may assure ourselves that this actually happened by reading his *Euthydemus*, where he puts into the mouths of two sophists some twenty arguments which he obviously believes to be fallacies. The *Euthydemus* as a whole is a copious, vivid, concrete picture of fallacious reasoning; and Plato evidently means it to be such.

But the *Euthydemus* as a whole, just because it is so *concrete*, does not settle the question what *abstract* consciousness Plato had of fallacy. It remains to be determined whether he had any word as abstract as the English word 'fallacy', and whether he distinguished various kinds of fallacy. Let us therefore inquire first into his consciousness of the generic notion of fallacy as such, and then into his consciousness of each of our four kinds of fallacy in turn.

When we search for names or definitions of the generic notion of fallacy, we are led to the conclusion that Plato has no word or phrase that means 'fallacy' as distinct from other forms of intellectual shortcoming. Such a phrase as πάντα ὅσα διανοίᾳ σφαλλόμεθα (*Soph.* 229C) includes every failure to grasp reality, and does not distinguish fallacy from falsehood. Nearest to it come his words 'alogon' and 'eristical' and 'antilogical' and 'sophistical'; but each of these means some larger complex in which the notion of fallacy is only an element not yet abstracted from the rest. 'Alogon' indicates the general notion of irrationality, including perverse behaviour. 'Eristical' and 'antilogical' are names for a whole type of philosophical or pseudo-philosophical behaviour, characterized especially by contentiousness and the tendency to contradict. 'Sophistical' is a still larger complex of notions with a strongly personal flavour. Even Aristotle expresses the notion of fallacy only by unsatisfactory phrases such as 'sophistical refutation', 'it does not syllogize', and 'there is no conclusion'.

If we look for some passage discussing the notion of fallacy as such, so far as that can be done without the aid of a name, we are again disappointed. Plato's dialogues have not made the abstraction of fallacy as such. They have not gone farther than the concrete presentation of particular fallacies, as found especially in the *Euthydemus*. Let us turn to our four species of fallacy, and ascertain whether the process of abstraction has risen as far as them in the dialogues.

(1) The *Euthydemus* (300C) contains a *question* that Plato obviously knows to be fallacious, although he makes no comment thereon. 'What, said Ctesippus, are not all things silent?—No, indeed, said Euthydemus.—Then all things are speaking, my dear man?—Those that are speaking.—That is not what I am asking, said he; I am asking you whether all things are speaking or silent?' In the *Gorgias* (503A) the answerer says 'that is not a simple question'. He does not mean that it is hard, but that the answer is 'sometimes yes and sometimes no'. Simplicity here means universality; a question is simple if we can answer it with a universal proposition, either affirmative or negative, but not simple if we have to descend to particulars and distinguish them. Earlier in the same dialogue (466CD) the answerer declares that the questioner is asking two questions at once. These passages give the measure of the insight expressed in the dialogues into the fact of fallacious question. They do not

amount to much. Even Aristotle recognizes this fallacy only in a special case, which is not very representative of its essence. He calls it 'making several questions into one' (*S.E.* 4, 166b27); and he never shows any realization that there is no such thing as a single question in the sense of a question that makes no assumption. His partial and atypical insight is embodied in the usual names 'complex question' or 'many questions'; and so far as I know the earliest person to see further was Lotze. The dialogues are roughly in Aristotle's stage, except that they have no conventional name for the thing.

(2) There are many passages in which the answerer's reply to Socrates' question is what we might call the rejection of an *analogy*. 'Some painters are better than others, presumably? —Certainly.—Now do the better ones produce finer works, that is, paintings? And in the same way do some architects make finer houses than others?—Yes.—Then is it also true that some lawgivers produce finer work than others?—No, I do not think so in this case' (*Cra.* 429AB). Very often the words used are that this is 'not like' that. 'I somehow feel, Socrates,' says Meno, 'that this is no longer like these others' (*Meno*, 73A). 'As if this were like that' is the contemptuous phrase with which Thrasymachus accuses Socrates of a false analogy (*Rp.* I, 337C). Once it is expressed by the proverb: 'You are joining flax and not-flax' (*Euthyd.* 298C). The *Charmides* (165E) has: 'You are not going about it in the right way, Socrates. This is not like the other forms of knowledge, nor are they like each other; but you are proceeding as if they were alike.' But we find no name for the fallacy, and no discussion of the conditions that tend to make an analogy false or true. Nor, as I show in my *Plato's Earlier Dialectic*, do we find any very explicit discussion of analogy in general. Plato's word ἀναλογία always means something strictly mathematical to him.

(3) As to fallacious *conversion*, Socrates points out in the

Euthyphro (12) that, whereas all that is holy is just, not all that is just is holy. He illustrates this by remarking that, whereas all that is reverenced is feared, not all that is feared is reverenced. The reason is, he says, that the fearful is wider than the reverend, that fear is a part of reverence. In this passage Plato grasps the notion of fallacious conversion to the extent that he can give two concrete cases of it, and place them side by side so that by comparison we may feel the universal nature present in them both; but he has no general name for this universal nature.

Exactly the same stage of insight reappears in the *Protagoras*:

You asked me whether brave men are confident, and I admitted it. But whether confident men are also brave I was not asked, and if I had been I should have said that they are not all so. My admission was that brave men are confident, and you have done nothing to show that it was wrong. You point out that those who know have more confidence than those who do not, and you think that proves that bravery and knowledge are the same. You could prove in this way that strength is knowledge. You could ask me first whether strong men are powerful, and I should say yes. Then, whether those who know how to wrestle are more powerful than those who do not, and more powerful than they themselves were before they learned, and I should say yes. And when I had made these admissions it would be possible for you, using the same proof, to say that according to my admissions knowledge is strength. But I am not for a moment admitting that the powerful are strong, only that the strong are powerful. For power and strength are not identical. Power comes both from knowledge and from madness and anger, while strength comes from nature and from good care of bodies. Similarly, in the other argument, confidence and bravery are not identical. Whence it happens that, while brave men are confident, not all confident men are brave. For confidence comes to men both from skill and from anger and from madness, like power, whereas bravery comes from nature and good care of souls. (350–1.)

Here as in the *Euthyphro* we are given concrete insight into the nature of fallacious conversion by being invited to see the identity in two juxtaposed cases of it; but we are not given any name or definition of this identical element. There are no other passages that express as much consciousness of the thing as these two.

(4) That Plato was sometimes conscious of the fallacy of *ambiguous terms* is certain from the *Euthydemus*, where he first makes the brothers commit this fallacy in a crass form with the word μανθάνειν, and then makes Socrates explain at length that the argument works by taking this word in two senses. Moreover, Plato comes nearer to having a name for ambiguity than to having names for fallacious question and analogy; for in this passage of the *Euthydemus* he calls it 'the difference of words' (τὴν τῶν ὀνομάτων διαφοράν 278B), and elsewhere he once has the word 'amphibolous' (*Cra.* 437A). Only on these two occasions, however, does he almost give a name to ambiguity. He often uses the word 'homonymous', but never in Aristotle's sense of a species of ambiguity.

This survey of Plato's consciousness of our four species of fallacy shows that it was very small. There is no discussion of fallacious question or analogy, only one passage discussing ambiguity, and only two discussing illegitimate conversion. The discussions of conversion juxtapose cases, but extract no name or definition. The only trace of names for any of the four are two names for ambiguity, each appearing once only.

We have now obtained a preliminary answer to our question what consciousness Plato had of fallacy. This answer is at present a mere sketch, very incomplete and yet at the same time too definite. It treats the problem too much as an affair of all or nothing. The assumption that Plato either was or was not aware of the notion of fallacy, and that there is no middle possibility between these two extremes, ought to be replaced by the assumption that a given man's awareness of any given conception can vary indefinitely in degree.

There is no such thing as a complete grasp of an idea; and there is no such thing as a zero grasp of an idea; and between any two degrees in the grasp of a given idea are others. On this assumption the comparatively simple question whether So and So had realized such and such idea must be replaced by the much harder question to what degree he had realized it. We have no established scale for such degrees, and therefore our answer to such a question can only consist in a long and laborious accumulation, piling up descriptions of the stage of the idea in this thinker, and comparisons of it with other thinkers. In the rest of this article we shall attempt this process for one species of fallacy only, namely, ambiguity. The choice of this species is indicated both by its frequency in the dialogues, and by its importance in philosophy, and by the fact that, unlike our other three species, it cannot be explained away as a falsehood in the premiss.

It is probable that all language is ambiguous, for it is probable that no statement whatever is or can possibly be accurate enough for all the purposes that may arise. In Whitehead's words, 'any verbal form of statement which has been before the world for some time discloses ambiguities; and . . . often such ambiguities strike at the very heart of the meaning'. But if all statements are ambiguous, much more so are all words; for a word as such is vaguer than a statement as such, and gains definition on each occasion from the sentence in which it appears. And we must understand the word 'ambiguous' to mean not merely meaning two things but meaning an indefinite number of things. All language is ambiguous, then, in the sense that every sentence and every word has an indefinite number of meanings; and the range of these meanings is usually much wider for words than for sentences.

We have already noticed a reason for believing that Plato had some consciousness of ambiguity; but we now require some more special reasons indicating that he realized to some extent the peculiar subtlety and formidableness of this type of fallacy. The passage in the *Euthydemus* is no evidence for this; it is one of those crass ambiguities out of which puns are made.

In the first place, there is an argument from the general character of the early dialogues. Shorey remarked that the *Lysis* 'reads precisely as if its philosophic purpose were to illustrate the mental confusion that arises when necessary and relevant distinctions are overlooked or not clearly brought out' (*What Plato Said*, p. 115). It is surely true that the great and salutary lesson the early dialogues have for us is ambiguity and again ambiguity—that our ordinary moral terms are profoundly ambiguous and confused. Is it possible to study these works philosophically without carrying away this conclusion, without deciding that we must not do what Socrates is always doing there, namely taking common terms into philosophy at their face value? If these works really drive home this important conclusion, is it not what Plato meant them to do? A book is a machine to think with, as I. A. Richards has said; and Plato's early dialogues are admirably designed to stimulate us into thinking.

In the second place, we may point to the discussion of λόγος at the end of the *Theaetetus*, and urge that Plato is there distinguishing three senses of the word. Λόγος, he says, is either the reflection of thought in words (206D), or the recital of the elements of a thing (206E ff.), or the statement of a mark that distinguishes the thing from everything else (208C). The discussion is elaborate and selfconscious.

In the third place, we may appeal to the discussion of not-being in the *Sophist*. Shorey, for example, there finds Plato 'explicitly distinguishing the copula from the substantive *is*' (*WPS*, 298). Surely, we may say, the following passage is the detection of a subtle ambiguity in the verb 'to be':

Let no one say that we are presuming to assert the being of not-being represented as the opposite of being. We have long ago said goodbye to the question whether there is any opposite of being or not, either explicable or completely inexplicable. But as to our present account of not-being, let a man either refute it and convince us that we are wrong, or, so long as he cannot, let him say as we do that the kinds mingle with each other; and that, since being and the other traverse all of them and each other, the other shares in being and *is* because of this sharing, while yet it *is not* that in which it shares, but, being other than being, is clearly necessarily not-being. (*Sophist*, 258E–259A.)

And surely the following is the detection of a subtle ambiguity in the phrase '. . . is the same':

We must overcome our distaste and admit that motion is both the same and not the same. For we are not speaking similarly when we call it the same and not the same, etc. (*Sophist*, 256A.)

Fourthly, we may appeal to the distinction drawn in the *Statesman* between a part and a kind or species or form. Plato there says (262–3) that it would be a mistake to divide animals into men and beasts, because 'beast' is only a part of 'animal' and not also a kind of animal. That this is a way of indicating that 'beast' is an ambiguous word appears strongly from the following sentence: 'You seemed to me to be merely subtracting a part, but to suppose that all that were left constituted a single kind because you could apply to each of them the same word "beast"' (263C). Plato here clearly indicates his opinion that the fact that we apply the same word 'beast' to each of a set of things is no guarantee that there is some 'form' common and peculiar to this set. This amounts to a recantation of his earlier belief that we could safely posit a 'form' wherever there was a common word (*Rp.* 596A). In other words, whereas in the middle dialogues the theory of 'forms' included the naïve assumption that most words are univocal, Plato is now beyond that stage, and realizes that we must do more than trust to language in order to discover 'forms'.

As a fifth and last argument, for the view that Plato appreciated the pervasiveness of ambiguity, we may remark that he had a pupil whose contribution to the study of ambiguity was certainly the most original ever made, and is probably still the best. In at least four different ways Aristotle advanced this matter enormously. He persistently noted and analysed and listed the various meanings of important philosophical terms. We have a substantial collection of these analyses in *Metaphysics Δ*; and they enter intimately into the texture of all his ontology. In the second place, he introduced illuminating descriptions of the various kinds of ambiguity. Thirdly, he listed six forms of fallacy dependent on language; and all of these are in reality forms of ambiguity, as he implies when he says that they are the ways in which we mean different things by the same words and sentences (*SE*, 4, 166b29). The most important of them is the fallacy caused by what he calls the σχῆμα λέξεως or grammatical form. He points out that we use one grammatical or syntactical device to express many different realities, and that we use more than one grammatical device to express a single reality. This concept of the absence of one-one correspondence between the grammatical structure and the object, even in true statements, leads directly to his greatest achievement of all in this sphere, the famous doctrine of the categories, which is the theory that being is an ambiguous word with ten different meanings. In this theory the pervasiveness of ambiguity is clearly suggested for the first time; for it means that the basic linguistic formula 'X is Y' has a different meaning for every category to which X may belong. It is a great pity that Aristotle did not elaborate the concept of analogical ambiguity mentioned in the *Nicomachean Ethics*, I, 6. It is a great pity that he has not left us a full-dress treatise on ambiguity as such, something more general than *Metaphysics Δ* and the *Categories*, and something less bound up with questions of controversy than the *Sophistical Refutations*. But surely, it may be argued, what he has given us justifies us in believing that his teacher saw more of ambiguity than any punster must.

Such are the arguments that can be made in favour of the view that Plato appreciated the seriousness of ambiguity. Turning to those on the other side, we may begin by rejecting the argument (number one above) that Plato must have intended the early dialogues to enforce the lesson of ambiguity. Surely the degree of irony thus attributed to him is superhuman. Do these dialogues suggest important truths about ambiguity to more than a tenth of the people who read them? Did they to more than a tenth of the readers whom Plato expected? We may doubt whether many Greeks could have profited by them in this way until Aristotle had done his work. It is easier for us than for them to see ambiguity in these dialogues, not only because we have Aristotle behind us, but also because we look at them from another language in which the ambiguities are different.

A second consideration strongly supporting the view that Plato was mostly unconscious of the subtler forms of ambiguity is stated in an article on ambiguity (*Mind*, l, 140–1), but had better be repeated here. In the typical procedure both of the early and of the middle dialogues there is a point where it is very important that the question of ambiguity should arise; and it never does. The typical procedure of the early dialogues is that Socrates puts a question of definition, the answerer misunderstands it and Socrates explains it, the answerer gives an answer, Socrates refutes it, the answerer gives another answer, Socrates refutes that, and so on. The question of ambiguity should arise before the question of definition. Before asking for the definition of X we should ask whether X always means the same; at least we should remember the possibility that X does not always mean the same during our search for its definition. In the *Meno* (74D) Socrates says to Meno: 'Since you give the same name to each of this multitude of things', what is the one element that you find in all of them? He does not raise the apparently prior question whether we give the same name to each of the collection in the same sense. The essence of the Socratic search for definitions is the insistence that the word *must* somehow mean the same in all its uses, however various they at first sight appear.

In the middle dialogues the typical procedure is to find an Idea wherever there is a common name. It is clearly expressed in the *Republic*: 'we are accustomed to assume that there is some one Idea related to each collection of things to which we give the same name' (596A). Evidently this is the same mistake in method as that with regard to definition in the early dialogues. We ought to bear in mind the possibility that the name is ambiguous; but the dialogues never do.

Against supposing Plato conscious of the subtleties of ambiguity we probably ought to put, thirdly, his contempt for those who seem to him to concern themselves with words instead of thoughts. Again and again he laughs at Prodicus for distinguishing closely related meanings; and one of these passages is specially interesting (*Euthd.* 277E) because it perhaps implies that Prodicus used to lay down the principle that you must learn about verbal correctness first, where first presumably means before you can learn about things. In the *Gorgias* he scorns what he calls word-hunting (489B and 490A). In the *Cratylus* he lays it down that the study of words is not the way to a knowledge of things. In the *Euthydemus* Socrates says that, even if a man knew many ambiguities such as μανθάνειν, or all there are, he would be no nearer knowing the truth about reality. In *Republic*, I, the notion of strict speech is introduced by an unsympathetic character as a desperate defence of an unsympathetic doctrine. Plato seems to hold the opinion, common also today, that we should despise nicety in the use of words, or at any rate intellectual as opposed to aesthetic nicety; that the truly original and liberal thinker attends only to things. The unnoticed implication seems to be that the good thinker can think correctly whatever words he uses as his symbols; and that he can understand what you are communicating to him however haphazardly you use your words. Such an attitude surely involves serious misapprehensions about the nature of language and our dependence thereon. No one maintains it after he has seen the range and power of ambiguity; and its presence in Plato is therefore a sign that he had not. The force of this argument is, however, somewhat lessened by the fact that Plato's utterances about language include many of another sort. The passages about the folly or difficulty or even impossibility of writing philosophy down seem to express a despair about words very different from the careless confidence implied in the passages we have just been recalling. Can it be that he thought that on the one hand communication by the written word is so precarious as to be hopeless, but on the other hand communication by the spoken word is so sure that elaborate precautions are needless?

Against the argument from Aristotle (number five above) we may say that Aristotle seems to forget his doctrines of ambiguity when he comes to ethics, and ethics is Plato's preponderating subject. The *Nicomachean Ethics* does, it is true, begin by declaring that good is an ambiguous word; but this doctrine does not permeate the book as the ambiguity of being permeates the *Metaphysics*; on the contrary, it is impossible to see any respect in which the rest of the book would have been different if he had not laid down this doctrine at the beginning. On the word ἀρετή, which is much more important to the book than the word good, he casts almost no suspicion; and most remarkable of all is his uncritical attitude to the word καλόν. This word is essential to his account of right action, for it is frequently invoked as being what the really virtuous man really aims at. Yet it is never related to happiness or to contemplation, both of which are also said to be the end; and it is never examined or discussed as such in any way. If, then, even Aristotle, who has so many and such good things to say on ambiguity, seems to forget the whole matter when he talks on ethics, we can perhaps easily believe that Plato did not have it in mind in his ethical dialogues. Throughout the history of philosophy ethics seems to have resisted the resolution of its terms much more than the other disciplines.

With regard to the second argument above, it is hard to say whether in the *Theaetetus* Plato is distinguishing three meanings of the word *logos*, or three species of the genus *logos*, or three hypotheses as to what the one thing *logos* is. *Logos*, he says, may be the reflection of thought in speech (206D), or the recital of the elements of a thing (206E ff.), or the statement of a mark that distinguishes the thing from everything else (208C). In favour of supposing that he regarded this as a case of ambiguity we observe that it is hard to see how the first could be either a co-species or a rival hypothesis to the other two. We observe also certain phrases that make this way. 'What does he mean by [the word] "logos"?' is probably a correct translation of τί ποτε βούλεται τόν λόγον ἡμῖν σημαίνειν; (206C, cf. Lewis Campbell *ad loc*). And the next sentence seems to be: 'For it seems to me to mean one of three things.' Ἴσως γὰρ ὁ λέγων οὐ τοῦτο ἔλεγεν (206E) probably means 'The man who asserted this definition perhaps did not mean this.' Thus Plato's language in introducing his first and second accounts of logos suggests that he thought he was dealing with an ambiguous word. On the other hand, what he says about his third account suggests rather that he thought he was dealing with rival hypotheses.

Perhaps someone will define it not thus, but as the remaining kind of the three, one of which, we said, will be laid down to be logos by him who defines knowledge as right opinion with logos. —You did right to remind us. Yes, there's one left. One was an image as it were of thought in speech. The other that we just mentioned was a path to the whole through the elements. And what is your third?—What most people would say; being able to name a mark by which the subject of inquiry differs from all things.

Here the phrase 'what most people would say', and the verb θήσεσθαι or 'lay down', with its close connection with ὑποτίθεσθαι or 'hypothesize', suggest that Plato thinks he is dealing with rival theories about the nature of the one thing logos.

These conflicting appearances indicate the following view of the passage. Plato here is not clearly separating the discrimination of the senses of an ambiguous word from the discrimination of theories about the nature of a thing. He passes from the former to the latter without realizing it. His second and third accounts of logos are rival attempts to clarify the nature of some one thing vaguely felt; but his first account refers to another thing altogether. Therefore, in passing from his first to his second account he is passing from one to another sense of an ambiguous word; but in passing from the second to the third he is passing not to a third sense, but only to a second hypothesis about the thing meant by the second sense. If this is the right interpretation, the discussion of logos in the *Theaetetus* is by no means a clear case of the detection of an ambiguity. It is an obscure detection of an ambiguity not distinguished from a perception of rival hypotheses.

The strongest of the arguments in favour of Plato's realizing the ambiguity of language were the appeals to the *Sophist* and the *Statesman*; and to these let us now turn.

With regard to the *Sophist*, we note that at best Plato is here dealing only with one or two cases of ambiguity, namely 'is not' and 'is the same'. The *Sophist* cannot by any stretch of the imagination be considered a discussion of ambiguity as such. It contains no word or phrase to which any dictionary would give the English equivalent 'ambiguity', nor any other of the related set of semantic terms, such as 'univocity' and 'meaning'. It does not even contain, in the passages to which the argument appeals, the word 'word' or ὄνομα. Translators make Plato much more precise than he was, and much more of a semanticist, when they render ὁμοίως by 'in the same sense', or οὕτως by 'in this sense', or ἐκείνη by 'the precise sense'. (The examples are from Cornford's translation of *Soph.* 256A, 256E, 259D.)

The fact is that, however the *Sophist* may seem to us, it did not seem to Plato to be a discussion of words or syntax or anything verbal at all. It seemed to him to be about the 'ideas' or 'forms', which, far from being human words, are realities very remote from man and quite independent of him. What appears to us as the discovery of the copula, a piece of grammar or logic, appeared to Plato as the discovery of a certain 'form', namely the Other, which has the wonderful property of 'communicating' with all other 'forms' without exception. In our language, he thought of his discussion of not-being as pure ontology, and not at all as semantics or logic. He is talking about Being, not the word 'being'; about the Other, not the word 'other'; about Forms or kinds, εἴδη or γένη, not about words or ὀνόματα. Hence Shorey and Taylor are mistaken in ascribing to him the discovery of the copula; and Cornford, although he denies this, is equally mistaken in finding that Plato here distinguishes meanings of 'is' and 'is not'.

Why is it, then, that so many interpreters find logical or grammatical doctrines in this part of the *Sophist*? The answer seems to be this. Suppose that I give you an account of Hans Pluke, describing at length his appearance, activities, relatives, and so on; suppose further that everything I say is true of one and the same existent individual, except that this individual's name is not Hans Pluke; suppose lastly that there never has been and never will be a man bearing the name of Hans Pluke. The three things thus supposed could jointly occur; they are each possible and together compossible.

This is an analogy of Plato's procedure in the *Sophist*. He there gives us an account of what he calls the 'form' of the Other; there is no such 'form'; nevertheless, all that he says about it is true of something else, namely the word 'other'. Not provided with any semantic concepts, and misconceiving the ontological status of his subject-matter, Plato has yet contrived to get wonderfully near to certain facts about language. Using extremely inappropriate tools, he has yet produced such a recognizable result that we all instinctively restate it for him in the more suitable language now available.

If this is a true account, the *Sophist* is so to speak almost but not quite at the top of the ridge that looks down into the valley of ambiguity. It is much higher than Plato ever climbed before, for it leaves far below the discussion of λόγος in the *Theaetetus*.

It is also higher than he ever reached again, with the possible exception of the passage from the *Statesman* put forward above as the fourth argument for the view that Plato saw the pervasiveness of ambiguity. This passage in the *Statesman* (262–3) is much less thorough and elaborate than that in the *Sophist*. Nevertheless, it comes nearer to formulating the idea of ambiguity as such. If Plato had confined himself to saying that a part is distinct from a 'form', the passage would have been little to our purpose; but, when he interprets this doctrine as implying that the existence of the word W is not sufficient evidence of the existence of a 'form' common and peculiar to all the things called W, we are strongly inclined to feel that, if only he had had at that moment some such word as ἀμφιβολία to provide a spark, a very bright flame would have been generated. As it is, however, the remarkable hint thrown out in this passage did not, so far as we know, lead to any revision of the theory of 'forms'; and Plato appears to have remained till death at the point of view stated in the *Euthydemus*, that ambiguity is of no importance to the philosopher.

3

FORMS AND ERROR IN PLATO'S
THEAETETUS

(*First printed in* The Philosophical Review *in 1950*)

THIS article examines two aspects of Plato's *Theaetetus*, first its relation to the theory of Forms, and second its discussion of error.

I

The theory of Forms is not conspicuous in the *Theaetetus*. The words '$\epsilon\hat{\iota}\delta o \varsigma$' and '$\iota\delta\acute{\epsilon}a$' occur (e.g. 184D, 203C–205D) but never seem to have the same technical sense which they sometimes obviously had in the *Phaedo* and the *Republic*. Other phrases which the middle dialogues also used to indicate Forms, such as '$o\dot{\upsilon}\sigma\acute{\iota}a$', '$a\dot{\upsilon}\tau\grave{o}\ \delta\iota$' $a\dot{\upsilon}\tau\acute{o}$', and '$\ddot{\epsilon}\nu$' as opposed to '$\pi o\lambda\lambda\acute{a}$', also occur in the *Theaetetus*, but no longer in such a way as to indicate that Plato is obviously referring to that theory. There is little or no talk about two worlds. Socrates does not mention now any of those thrilling attributes, such as eternity and divinity, which in the middle dialogues had made the Forms objects of worship and love. There is no question now of openly using the theory of Forms as a premiss for the deduction of important conclusions in the way in which the *Phaedo* used it to deduce that soul is immortal.

Two doctrines which the middle dialogues had closely associated with the theory of Forms are also conspicuously absent from the *Theaetetus*, namely recollection and the absolute difference of knowledge from opinion. As to recollection, to take that first, there is indeed one Platonist who finds it several times in the *Theaetetus*, namely Léon

Robin;[1] but I know of nobody who agrees with him, and all of his references seem certainly wrong. He finds it, for example, when Socrates ends his refutation of the theory that knowledge is sense by urging that there are some things which 'the soul herself by herself' examines without any help whatever from the senses (185CD). Of course the phrase 'herself by herself' is reminiscent of the language in which the middle dialogues stated the theory of Forms, but it can justify us in finding the doctrine of recollection in the *Theaetetus* only if we assume that anything that reminds us of the theory is equivalent to an assertion of it along with its attachments. The same argument includes the statement that 'whereas the sensations that reach the soul through the body can by nature be perceived by men and beasts as soon as they are born, reflections on these things with regard to their essence and utility come to those to whom they come at all only with difficulty and after much training and trouble' (186BC). This was an opportunity to reassert the doctrine of recollection, but Socrates is not made to do so.

In one of the passages in which Robin found recollection, namely the comparison of the soul to an aviary, I find rather the opposite. Socrates says that when we were children our aviaries were empty (197E); on the theory of recollection I think he should rather have said that the aviary is full from birth, but until we are grown up and have had training we are unable to catch in our hands the birds that we have in our cages. The comparison of the soul to a waxen tablet also seems out of harmony with the doctrine of recollection, although Socrates does not say that the tablet is blank at birth.

The *Theaetetus* is the dialogue in which Socrates compares himself to a midwife, that image which has so gripped our minds that we usually think of it as a feature of all the Socratic literature and of the real Socrates. But what is the

[1] *Platon*, pp. 72, 88.

relation of this image to the doctrine of recollection? Robin is quite wrong in saying that Socrates is made to base his midwifery on recollection. On the contrary, the children of which Socrates delivers Theaetetus cannot be Forms, because they may be false; and by the doctrine of recollection Socrates should be fertile himself, instead of being barren as he says he is. I have no hesitation in saying that the doctrine of recollection is never referred to in the *Theaetetus* and that the general tone of the dialogue is rather against it.

The theory that knowledge is radically distinct from opinion is another important attachment to the theory of Forms in the middle dialogues. The *Theaetetus*, however, takes very seriously the suggestion that knowledge is precisely true opinion with logos; and, though the suggestion is rejected, it is not rejected by an appeal to the doctrine of the *Republic*. The earlier suggestion, that knowledge is true opinion in general, was rejected by an argument that seems actually to deny the *Republic*'s view. We are told that knowledge cannot be just true opinion because jurymen sometimes achieve a true opinion about events which only an eyewitness could know about, περὶ ὧν ἰδόντι μόνον ἔστιν εἰδέναι (201B), and this seems to imply that we can sometimes know through our eyes and know an event in this changing world, whereas the *Republic* held that there is knowledge only of the invisible Forms. It is a fascinating question, on which I have not yet been able to make up my mind, whether this is a slip or an unnoticed implication on Plato's part. But there are other parts of the *Theaetetus* which also seem to imply that there can be knowledge of the sensible world. We are told that some things the soul considers through the body (185E); and there is talk of particular persons and things as if they were possible objects of knowledge. The discussion of the waxen tablet seems to contemplate the possibility of knowing particular persons, and the discussion of the last theory of knowledge seems to contemplate the possibility of defining, and therefore knowing, that particular sensible thing, the sun (208D).

The general atmosphere of the dialogue seems unfavourable to the theory of Forms. I do not mean the almost total absence of religious tone, for the theory of Forms of the middle dialogues was a scientific as well as a religious doctrine; its immense value was precisely that it appeared to satisfy the demands of religion and of science both. What seems definitely unfavourable to the theory of Forms is the empiricist and subjectivist tone of the *Theaetetus*. It contains the first, or first surviving, statement of the great empiricist comparison of the mind to a waxen tablet. It makes Socrates say that 'human nature is too weak to have science of that which it has not experienced' (149C). And, as I have just said in another connection, it often seems to imply knowledge of the things of experience. By its 'subjectivism' I mean that it allows the theory, that whatever seems so to a man is so to him, to come on the scene and be developed at length, and that it turns away from the objective world of Forms to deal with our thinking, our fallibility, and our sensations.

Is the inconspicuousness of the Forms in the *Theaetetus* due to Plato's not having believed in them when he wrote it? The answer yes was easy to accept in the days before stylometry, when one could hold that the *Theaetetus* was an early dialogue, written before the theory of Forms was thought of and expressed in the *Phaedo* and the *Republic*. But it is far more difficult to say yes now that we are all convinced that the *Theaetetus* and the *Parmenides* were both written shortly before Plato's first visit to the court of Dionysius II and well after the *Republic* and the *Phaedo*. Can we somehow make it seem reasonable that Plato should have in 368 written a dialogue which appears to coldshoulder his famous theory?

An interesting attempt to do this has been made by the late Professor Cornford in his book, *Plato's Theory of Knowledge*.

The essence of his view is that the absence of the Forms from the *Theaetetus* is a deliberate device to show that we cannot get on without them.[1] I will first describe and then examine Cornford's development of this view.

Cornford held that

> The *Theaetetus* [formulates and examines] the claim of the senses to yield knowledge. The discussion moves in the world of appearance and proves that, if we try to leave out of account the world of true being, we cannot extract knowledge from sensible experience.[2]

> The theory of Anamnesis . . . cannot be mentioned in the *Theaetetus*, because it presupposes that we know the answer to the question here to be raised afresh: What is the nature of knowledge and of its objects? For the same reason all mention of the Forms is, so far as possible, excluded. The dialogue is concerned only with the lower kinds of cognition, our awareness of the sense-world and judgements involving the perception of sensible objects. . . . The Forms are excluded in order that we may see how we can get on without them; and the negative conclusion of the whole discussion means that, as Plato had taught ever since the discovery of the Forms, without them there is no knowledge at all.[3]

When Cornford comes to the interlude on the difference between the philosopher and the lawyer (*Tht.* 172–7), he says it is an indirect reply to the view that what is right has no natural existence at all.

> A direct treatment would demand a repetition of the contents of the *Republic* and arguments supporting the Platonic thesis that the moral Forms, Justice, and the rest, do 'exist by nature with a being of their own'. But the Forms are to be excluded, so far as possible, from this conversation, which discusses the claim of the world of appearances to yield knowledge without invoking the

---

[1] Professor Cherniss expressed the same view briefly in his article, "The Philosophical Economy of the Theory of Ideas', *American Journal of Philology*, 1936.

[2] Cornford, p. 7.   [3] Ibid., p. 28.

intelligible world. So Plato is content to indicate his answer by reviving the contrast drawn in the *Gorgias* and the *Republic* between the orator of the lawcourt or the Assembly and the true statesman, the philosopher whose knowledge lies in that other realm of reality. The whole digression is studded with allusions to the *Republic*, and in the course of it the moral Forms are plainly, though unobtrusively, mentioned.[1]

Cornford finds 'a clear allusion to the theory of Forms' in the statement that the philosopher hardly knows whether his neighbour is a man but is at pains to discover 'what is man and what it befits such a nature to do or suffer in distinction from other things' (*Tht.* 174B). And he finds that the moral Forms are openly mentioned and that there are allusions to the *Republic*'s allegory of the Cave in Socrates' speech about the philosopher dragging the orator upwards 'to examine justice itself and injustice, what each of them is and how they differ from everything or from each other' (*Tht.* 175C).

From the refutation of Heracliteanism by means of the distinction between locomotion and alteration, Plato intends us, according to Cornford, to draw the conclusion that

Unless we recognize some class of knowable entities exempt from the Heracleitean flux and so capable of standing as the fixed meanings of words, no definition of knowledge can be any more true than its contradictory. Plato is determined to make us feel the need of his Forms without mentioning them.[2]

The conclusion would be more obvious if it were not his plan to exclude mention of the Forms.[3]

The final argument against the thesis that knowledge is sense is that the soul herself by herself knows existence and non-existence and such things as are 'common to all'. And 'that these "common" terms are Forms should', writes Cornford, 'be obvious to anyone who has read the *Parmenides*', though Plato here avoids using the word because he is determined to say as little about the Forms as possible.[4]

---

[1] Cornford, p. 83. [2] Ibid., p. 99. [3] Ibid., p. 101. [4] Ibid., p. 106.

The middle section of the *Theaetetus*, which deals with the problem of error, has for its aim, according to Cornford, 'to see how far we can get towards an explanation of false judgement without invoking the Forms'.[1] Its image of the waxen tablet does not mean that Plato has abandoned his doctrine of recollection; it represents the empiricist assumption whose adequacy Plato is examining and which he does not himself accept.[2] As to the next image, the aviary, 'the Platonist will see at once that what is here called a "piece of knowledge" can be nothing more than a belief. . . . All this cannot be openly said here, because the Forms are excluded from the discussion.'[3] The discussion of error ends inconclusively 'because he cannot go further without invoking the true objects of knowledge'. But in the *Sophist* the Forms are brought in again, and the problem of error is solved by them.[4]

The last section of the dialogue, the discussion of the thesis that knowledge is true opinion with logos, still proceeds, according to Cornford, on the assumptions

. . . that the only things to be known are concrete individual things, and that knowledge accordingly must consist in giving some account of such things. This limitation is in accordance with the scope of the whole dialogue, which asks whether knowledge can be extracted from the world of concrete natural things, yielding perceptions and complex notions, without invoking other factors. The three meanings of *logos* now considered are determined by these assumptions, which exclude Plato's own view, that the objects of which knowledge must give an account are not concrete individuals but objects of thought, and that the simpler terms in which the account must be stated are not material parts but higher concepts.[5]

[From the failure of the thesis] the Platonist will draw the necessary inference. True knowledge has for its object things of a different order—not sensible things, but intelligible Forms and truths about them.[6]

---

[1] Ibid., p. 111.   [2] Ibid., pp. 129–30.   [3] Ibid., p. 135.
[4] Ibid., p. 140.   [5] Ibid., p. 154.   [6] Ibid., p. 162.

By the phrase 'the Platonist' in this and other passages Cornford appears to have meant one who believes the doctrines of the *Meno*, *Phaedo*, *Symposium*, and *Republic*. This usage rather assumes that Plato went on believing in the theory of Forms to the end of his life.

I think that this view of Cornford's is not a true answer to the question why the Forms are so inconspicuous in the *Theaetetus*; and I will now give reasons for this judgement, first by considering Cornford's interpretation of particular parts of the dialogue, and then by some general remarks.

The first passage in which Cornford found the Forms hinted at is the contrasting of the philosopher with the orator (*Tht.* 172–7). This interlude is, I agree, more reminiscent of the *Republic* than any other part of the dialogue. It tells us that the philosopher is leisured and eleutheros, a theorist, totally uninterested in particulars and practical affairs, indifferent to ordinary values owing to his wide views, a fool to the masses, an imitator of God. This can all be well paralleled in the *Republic*, for the philosopher's being totally uninterested in practical affairs is consistent with the philosopher-king's taking his turn at ruling. But is every theorist and every imitator of God a believer in Forms? Surely the whole of this description, except for the imitation of God, could be truly said of a nominalist and positivist philosopher; for the essence of it is that the philosopher is a theorist, a generalizer, and a spectator of the whole. The two passages to which in particular Cornford appealed say no more than you could find Socrates saying in the early dialogues. To claim them as allusions to the theory of Forms is to make Shorey's mistake, that any request for a definition of the essence of justice itself is the theory of Forms. The theory of Forms is the theory that there is a second world, of objects which, unlike the objects here, have the attributes of being perfect, unchanging, eternal, divine, etc.; and this theory is not implied by the *Theaetetus*' description of the philosopher, though it is not denied by it either. Cornford speaks of the contrast between the philosopher and the orator as drawn in the *Gorgias* as well as in the *Republic*; but the *Gorgias* does not contain the theory of Forms.

The next part of the *Theaetetus* in which Cornford finds the theory of Forms suggested is the refutation of the fluxers by means of the distinction between locomotion and alteration. I feel quite sure that this is a mistake. What that argument professes to show is that the fluxers are wrong because they must, in order to be genuine fluxers, hold that everything is always changing both its position and also its character, but this view entails that nothing can have any description applied to it (*Tht.* 182D4), or all answers are equally right (*Tht.* 183A5), or all existing language is useless except perhaps the phrase 'not so' (*Tht.* 183B4). We are tacitly given to understand that these consequences are obviously false and therefore the view which entails them must be false too. The argument concludes by suggesting that the theory of universal fluxion, being false, offers no support for the theory that man is the measure of all things or for the theory that knowledge is sense (*Tht.* 183B7 ff.).

Why is this not enough? Why must we suppose that the consequences Plato made his characters draw are not all of the consequences he had in mind and wished his readers to draw? What reason have we to hypothesize an esoteric conclusion beyond, that would be grasped only by adept Platonists? I think we have none. The argument as explicitly stated seems to me excellent food for the philosophic mind just as it is, and just what the scheme of the dialogue demands. It is put forward as part of the refutation of the theory that has been constructed round the doctrine that knowledge is sense, and that is what it is.

But supposing that Plato had been doing what Cornford thought he was doing, namely inferring that the Forms exist, would it have been a valid inference? Surely not. The argument professes to show that there must be something stable somewhere. But it has no particular tendency to show that this stable something is the Forms, or any otherworldly object at all. On the contrary, what it shows is rather that there is something stable in *this* world. For a refutation of the proposition that everything *in this world* is always changing both its place and its character would be a proof of the proposition that something *in this world* is sometimes stable in respect of either its place or its character or both. Thus the train of thought which Cornford was attributing to Plato is an error, a fact which Cornford did not mention. This demonstration of our need for Forms by the method of withholding them would not succeed in so far as the reader was a clear thinker.

The next passage in which Cornford found the Forms was the proof that knowledge is not sense by appealing to the premiss that the soul does not use the senses at all in knowing existence and non-existence and things that are 'common to all' (*Tht.* 184 –6). These things that are 'common to all' are obviously Forms in Cornford's view. Whether they are Forms is not obvious to me, and to my mind depends rather on the dreadful question whether the μέγιστα γένη of the *Sophist* are Forms, on which I have not yet succeeded in reaching a confident opinion. But I think it quite possible that they are Forms.

In this case Cornford does not go on to say that Plato is implying that there are Forms by declining to mention them and showing what difficulties result. If Plato *does* mention Forms here, he cannot at the same time be trying to make them conspicuous by their absence.

I pass to the central section of the dialogue, which is mainly a discussion of error under the head of a discussion of the definition of knowledge as true opinion. Its aim according to Cornford is 'to see how far we can get towards an explanation of false judgement without invoking the Forms'.[1] And its inconclusive end is meant to signify to us that error is possible only because there are Forms. And in fact the later dialogue *Sophist* does solve the problem of error by bringing in the Forms.[2]

I dispute the whole of this interpretation, both as regards the *Theaetetus* and as regards the *Sophist*.

In the first place, I deny that the *Sophist* introduces the Forms into its explanation of error. I do so not on the basis that the Forms do not appear in the *Sophist* at all, since the μέγιστα γένη are not Forms (for on that point I cannot reach a settled opinion), but on the basis that neither the μέγιστα γένη nor any other possible disguise of the Forms enters into the actual explanation of error in that dialogue. It is true that this explanation, when being introduced, is tied to the discussion of the μέγιστα γένη by being represented as the question whether not-being ever blends with thinking and discourse (*Soph.* 260B); but this introduction is merely dramatic and 'dialectical', as Cornford remarks,[3] and does not correctly describe what actually happens in the explanation. The essence of Plato's explanation of error in the *Sophist* is this. Every logos is a compound of unlike parts. At the least it is a compound of one noun and one verb. It asserts that this thing, signified by its noun, has this attribute, signified by its verb. Each of its simple parts, noun or verb, signifies something real. The possibility of logos in general is given by this fact that each of its simple parts signifies something real. And the possibility of *false* logos is given by the fact that logos, being always compound, may assert that these realities are connected otherwise than as they are. And the possibility of false *thinking* is given by the fact that thought is nothing but inner logos. I believe that, if you read the passage (*Soph.* 261 –4), you will agree that this is a true account of its message and that it does not mention Forms.

[1] Cornford, p. 111.   [2] Ibid., p. 140.   [3] Ibid., p. 298.

Why then did Cornford say that the *Sophist* uses the Forms to solve the problem of error? He admits that Plato does not explicitly mention the Forms here, but he writes that he evidently means them to come in. I cannot give a full account of his reasons for this interpretation, for they involve two or three pages of obscure and so far as I can see irrelevant discussion. I can only report and consider the four brief arguments which he gives for his statement that 'Plato evidently means the Forms to come in'.[1]

First he says that 'the whole section on combination of Forms was avowedly to furnish the key to false statement'; and this is true, provided that the μέγιστα γένη *are* Forms. This is a strong argument, and on my view Plato does, by failing to make use of his previous discussion, disappoint an expectation which he has aroused. But such an apparent hiatus ought not to lead us to fill it from our own minds, and I personally find no echo in the text of the filling which Cornford offers.

Cornford's second consideration is that Plato 'has said that "all discourse depends on the weaving together of Forms" (259E), i.e. at least one Form enters into the meaning of any statement'. This again is true, provided that 'εἴδη' means Forms in that sentence; and again it helps to create an incoherence between our anticipations and the actuality. But again the incoherence does not justify, in my opinion, such a wholesale injection into the text as Cornford undertakes.

Cornford's third point is that in this passage Plato 'refers to statements made earlier about Forms: "in the case of everything there are many things that are, and also many that are not." This [Cornford remarks] was said of Forms in a context where individual things were not in question at all.' This argument has the same value as the first and second.

Cornford's fourth point is that 'we have seen that the failure of the *Theaetetus* to explain false statement was due to

---

[1] Cornford, p. 314.

the deliberate exclusion of Forms.' I maintain that we have seen only that *Cornford suggested* that the failure of the *Theaetetus* to explain false statement was due to this. Cornford had two hypotheses, one that the *Theaetetus'* discussion of error is meant to show that error cannot be explained without the Forms, and the other that the *Sophist's* discussion of error is meant to explain error by means of the Forms; and part of his argument for each of these hypotheses was to infer it from the other, which for the time being was assumed to be established.

That is all that I can do, without becoming boring, to reject Cornford's view that the *Sophist* is intended to explain error by means of the Forms. I will now assume that I have deprived him of the assistance of his theory of the *Sophist* in his attempt to interpret the *Theaetetus*, and consider what evidence there is left for his view that the *Theaetetus'* discussion of error is meant to show indirectly that error cannot be explained without the help of the Forms. It seems to me that *no* evidence is left. I do not find that Cornford in his comments on the *Theaetetus* introduces any evidence whatever for his statement that Plato 'breaks off here because he cannot go farther without invoking the true objects of knowledge',[1] excepting only the statement about the *Sophist* which I have just rejected.

Is it necessary to suppose that Plato meant us to infer *anything* from his discussion of error in the *Theaetetus*? Must the meaning of every great literary work be something that the author himself omitted to say? I think every practising philosopher feels profoundly delighted with the discussion as it is. But, if Plato *was* thinking of any ulterior effect on his readers, I think I know from his *Parmenides* and his *Phaedrus* the sort of effect it was. He probably said to himself something like this: 'Of course it is quite obvious that error *does* occur, and therefore it is quite certain that there is something

[1] Ibid., p. 140.

wrong with every argument that offers to prove that error *cannot* occur, and therefore I am giving to philosophers the delightful task of finding out what is wrong with these arguments.'

In the last pages of the *Theaetetus* there is an end of digressions about error and universal flux and sensation, and a concentrating on the ostensible question of the whole dialogue, what knowledge is. No satisfying answer is found. The best that can be thought of, namely that knowledge is true opinion with logos, is held to be wrong in all three senses of 'logos'.

Here again, according to Cornford, Plato meant us to think more than he writes. 'The Platonist will draw the necessary inference. True knowledge has for its object things of a different order—not sensible things, but intelligible Forms and truths about them.'[1] For the discussion proceeds throughout on the assumption that the only things to be known are concrete individuals and shows that if that is so knowledge cannot be defined, which in turn entails that knowledge is not of concrete individuals but of Forms.

This too I believe to be a mistake. The inference which Cornford here attributes to Plato is not valid. If knowledge of concrete individuals cannot be defined, it does not follow that there are Forms. Perhaps knowledge is indefinable, or perhaps there is no knowledge. However, Plato might of course have thought the inference valid.

But is it correct to say that what the passage primarily establishes is that knowledge of concrete individuals cannot be defined? Surely the arguments tend to show that knowledge cannot be defined as true opinion with logos no matter what we suppose its objects to be. And surely this is what Plato meant them to do. For example, the argument, to prove that knowledge is not just true opinion plus an account of the difference of the object from all other things, surely

[1] Cornford, p. 162.

remains just as strong if we suppose that the object in question is a Form. The argument proceeds by putting the question whether in knowing *x* we know or merely opine what it is that differentiates *x* from all else; for, if we know it, knowledge is being defined through itself, while, if we merely opine it, true opinion about *x* and its differentia does not seem to constitute knowledge. Surely this argument applies just as much when *x* is a Form.

Some passages of Cornford tend to give the impression that he was thinking that the arguments disprove these three definitions of knowledge as true opinion with logos only for cases where the object is a concrete thing, and if so he is liable to the above objection. But there are certainly other passages in which he meets the above objection by saying that Plato had in mind a fourth sense of 'logos' which he does not bring forward here.

Two questions arise about this fourth sense of 'logos'. The first is what it is, for strangely enough I cannot find that Cornford tells us, though he writes as if he knew. He tells us that it is to be found in the *Meno* and the *Timaeus*,[1] and he later refers to the servant in the *Meno* and his prospects of grasping a 'necessary connection';[2] but that is all, and it does not seem to tell us what the sense is.

The other question that arises about this supposed fourth sense of 'logos' is what is its relation to the question of the objects of knowledge. Cornford appears to be interpreting Plato here by means of two separate distinctions, namely the distinction between Forms as objects of knowledge and concrete individuals as objects of knowledge, and the distinction between the fourth sense of 'logos' and the other three. What is the relation between these two distinctions? Were they meant to coincide, so that one could not give the fourth sense to 'logos' without thereby implying that the objects of knowledge are and must be Forms? One wonders

[1] Ibid., p. 142.   [2] Ibid., p. 158.

whether Cornford was thinking that the fourth sense of 'logos' was that the logos of x is precisely the Form which x either is or imitates. He combines the two rather closely when he writes: 'The three meanings of *logos* now considered are determined by these assumptions, which exclude Plato's own view, that the objects of which knowledge must give an account are not concrete individuals but objects of thought, and that the simpler terms in which the account must be stated are not material parts but higher concepts.'[1] And when he writes that 'these senses appear to exhaust the possible ways in which an "account" can be given of an individual thing',[2] he seems to be hinting that when we suppose the object of knowledge to be the Forms, and not till then, we are able to think of a fourth sense of 'logos', and we then see that in this fourth sense the true definition of knowledge *is* that it is true opinion with logos.

One of the difficulties of the hypothesis that Plato thought he could define knowledge by means of a fourth sense of 'logos' is that he seems to imply in the *Theaetetus* that some knowable things have no logos at all. For the examination of the three senses of 'logos' is immediately preceded by a discussion of uncompounded elements, the tendency of which is to conclude that, if elements are unknowable because they have no logos, everything is unknowable, from which anyone who thought that knowledge does occur would have to conclude that a thing's being alogon does not make it unknowable. This seems to throw out the definition of knowledge as true opinion with logos no matter what sense we give to 'logos'.

I have gone through this tiresome little account of Cornford's doctrine that Plato had a fourth sense of 'logos' in the hope of recommending the opinion which I now state: Cornford entirely fails to make this doctrine probable. The turth is, in my opinion, that the discussion of logos at the end

[1] Cornford, p. 154.   [2] Ibid., p. 162.

of the *Theaetetus* is a small example of a certain Platonic procedure which we find on a larger scale elsewhere, namely a searching critique of one of Plato's own favourite doctrines, which he nevertheless continued to hold after writing the critique in spite of the fact that he does not appear ever to have discovered the answer to it. It was one of his firm convictions, from the *Meno* (αἰτίας λογισμός), or at any rate the *Republic* (534BC), down to the *Seventh Letter* (342B, etc.) and the *Timaeus* (51E), that knowledge entails logos. Yet here at the end of the *Theaetetus* he offers strong arguments to show that logos does not entail knowledge, and, much worse, that some aloga must be knowable if there is any knowledge at all. The larger example of this brilliant self-criticism is the discussion of Forms in the *Parmenides*. It is part of Plato's genius that, after having invented in his middle period a theory which is great enough to satisfy most people's philosophical urges for life, he went still farther and published extremely acute and candid objections to his theory. I do not believe that, either in the big matter of the Forms or in this little matter of logos, he had any solution of his own difficulties up his sleeve. I believe that he could not produce any other plausible senses of 'logos' than those he here dismisses.

It is noteworthy that his two main senses of 'logos' here, the elements of a thing and the differentia of a thing, correspond to the two main aspects of the Socratic 'What-is-*x*?' question in the early dialogues, for there Socrates tends to explain his question either as a demand for what differentiates *x* from all else or as a demand for the essence of *x*, and giving the essence of *x* tends to be analysing it into elements.

I conclude that Cornford failed to establish his interpretation for this last part of the dialogue also.

In general it is true to say that, if Plato intended the *Theaetetus* to demonstrate that sense cannot give knowledge and all knowledge is of the Forms, he made a poor job of it.

For what the dialogue ostensibly does is to show the inadequacy of all plausible definitions of knowledge. In addition to this main purpose it also refutes extreme Heracliteanism and relativism and urges very strongly that there is a serious difficulty in seeing how error is possible. And the inference from these ostensible conclusions to the ulterior conclusion, which Cornford says Plato intended his readers to draw, is esoteric and chancy. Furthermore, there are several statements in the dialogue which badly misfit this supposed ulterior conclusion. If Plato's aim was to convince us that sense has no part in knowledge, it was certainly unfortunate to admit, as Cornford thinks he does, that simple sensation is infallible, and to say, as he clearly does, that some things are perceived by the soul *through the senses* (*Tht.* 186) and to use an argument which implies that an eyewitness knows what he sees (*Tht.* 201). The implication that an eyewitness knows what he sees is also very unfortunate on the positive half of Cornford's interpretation, namely that the dialogue is intended to show that knowledge is of Forms only.

Does the difference between knowledge and true opinion lie in their objects or in their action or in both? The *Republic*, I think we may say, held that it lies in both, for faculties were distinguished there both by ἐφ' ᾧ ἐστιν and by ὃ ἀπεργάζεται (*Rp.* 477). Cornford's interpretation tends to imply that the *Theaetetus* regards the difference as lying only in their objects. He writes as if, once we admit that the object of knowledge is the Forms, we know what knowledge is. He does not contemplate the view that, however much we know that knowledge is of the Forms, we do not thereby know what knowledge is. He tends to regard the doctrine that knowledge is of the Forms as itself a definition of knowledge, the true definition of knowledge implied by the failure of all those explicitly mentioned. To me, on the contrary, the *Theaetetus* appears to take little or no interest in the enterprise of distinguishing knowledge from true opinion by means of its objects, because however much that might be done it would not give us that essence of knowledge which it is the aim of the dialogue to find. I think that at no time of Plato's life would he ever have regarded the statement that knowledge is about the Forms as the complete answer to the question what knowledge *is*. He never thought that knowledge was so to speak merely true opinion about Forms and that true opinion was so to speak merely knowledge about sensibles.

This concludes my account of the reasons why I think that Cornford has not given us the answer to the question why the Forms are so inconspicuous in the *Theaetetus*.

My own answer to the question is implied in what I have just said. The Forms are absent from the *Theaetetus* merely because they are irrelevant to the subject discussed there. The subject of the *Theaetetus* is the essence of knowledge, and the essence of knowledge is not the same as its object. If you are asked what a gun is, it is not the right answer to say what the gun is pointing at. If you are asked what knowledge is, it is not the right answer to say what its object is. Plato has here turned his attention away from the world of Forms to the mind of man. And why not? I venture to assert that to a practising philosopher nothing more than Plato's explicit discussion of the definition of knowledge is wanted to make the *Theaetetus* a fascinating dialogue. We do not need some metaphysics hinted at behind it all. We are entirely delighted with what is explicit, the keen and full development of the difficulty of defining knowledge. (There is indeed only one Platonic dialogue of which I admit that its lesson is something it does not say, and that is the enigmatic *Parmenides*. I think the lesson of the *Parmenides* is that we must practise ourselves very hard indeed in the scrutiny of arguments and the detection of fallacies; and this is not altogether stated in the dialogue, even in the short transitional passage about mental gymnastics.)

EEG

This account of the reason why the Forms do not appear in the *Theaetetus* would be compatible with saying that Plato no longer believed in the Forms when he wrote the dialogue. And something very like this bold suggestion was made by Professor Ryle in his articles on the *Parmenides*:

> It has long been recognized that in the whole period which includes the writing of the *Theaetetus*, the *Sophist*, the *Politicus*, and the *Philebus*, Plato's thinking is not entirely, if at all, governed by the premisses of the Theory of Forms. He attends to the theory on occasions, but he does so in a dispassionate and critical way.[1]

It is the fact that in *Parmenides*, *Theaetetus*, *Sophist*, *Statesman*, and *Philebus*, the only *obvious* references to the theory of Forms as found in the middle dialogues are the acute objections offered to it in the *Parmenides* and the *Sophist*. Passages which assume it or support it, if they exist, are certainly written in a new sort of language and are hard to recognize. It is the fact that these dialogues exhale a very different odour, no longer the religious and metaphysical devotion of the middle dialogues with their too simple and sweeping attitude towards logical problems, but rather the smell of books and desks and seminar-rooms.

Yet there are also very strong objections to the view that Plato has now abandoned the theory, namely that the tradition represents him as never abandoning it and that two other late dialogues clearly express it, the *Phaedrus* and the *Timaeus*. We must, I think, with von Arnim, suppose the *Phaedrus* to be later than the *Theaetetus*. The evidence of style makes it much later than the *Republic*; and the discussion of diaeresis and synagoge, which occupies a prominent position in the *Phaedrus*, forms a very close link to the *Sophist* and the *Statesman*, in each of which diaeresis is the secondary subject. It is possible that a re-examination of these dialogues might enable us to say that in them the theory

---

[1] *Mind*, 1939, p. 315.

of Forms has only a mythical, no longer a fully scientific, status. But, until such re-examinations have actually been made and such results produced, I hardly think it wise to go so far as to say that Plato did not believe in the theory of Forms at this period. What seems much more probable is that he at least still *thought* he believed in it, though in his active inquiries he was in fact beyond it, and it functioned as a theory to be criticized instead of as the rock of salvation it had been in his middle period.

II

I pass now to the discussion of error in the *Theaetetus*. The problem of error occupies about half of this dialogue. A fifth of it is explicitly devoted to error (pp. 187–200); and previously to this another third is really very largely concerned with it, namely the discussion of Protagoras' doctrine that man is the measure of all things, which is taken to imply that whatever seems so to anybody is so to him, which of course implies that error does not occur (pp. 152–79).

The development of the thesis, that knowledge is sense, into a complex which entails that error does not occur goes something like this. We commonly assume that each thing has a nature of its own, independent of all else, and that the sensible qualities are in things and form part of their independent nature. But from this it would follow that, if a thing is different now from what it was before, it must have changed in the interval, whereas Socrates, who was formerly taller than Theaetetus, is now shorter than he without having changed height; and six dice, which were *more* when we compared them with four, are *fewer* now when we compare them with twelve dice, although they have not changed their number (*Tht.* 154BC–155BC). Our common assumption that each thing has an independent nature of its own is therefore false, and sensible qualities are not permanent qualities of independent things. Nor are the sensible qualities parts of us. They are the products of the interaction of a sense-organ with a thing and exist between the two (*Tht.* 153D–154B). And this is true not merely of the sensible quality but also of our sensation of it. Each of them is a motion and a product of the interaction of our sense-organ with the thing. And they necessarily go together. The interaction of organ and thing always has a twin product, and the sensation and the sensible quality never occur apart (*Tht.* 156B1–2, 160A8–B3). Not merely are the sensation and the sensible quality motions, but the organ and the thing are motions too, though slower ones (*Tht.* 156CD); and everything in the world is in motion. If the wind seems hot to you and cold to me, the difference is due to the difference of the organs with which the wind is interacting. In fact, it *cannot* seem the same to me as it does to you, for a different organ *must* produce a different sensation and a different sensible (*Tht.* 160A). Every sensible is peculiar to a particular sensation, and conversely. And thus all sensation is necessarily true (*Tht.* 160C). Every one of my sensations inevitably gives me the actual sensible that is really caused by the interaction of my organ and the thing (*Tht.* 160C). The sensations of dreamers and madmen are just as true as any others. This doctrine is to be extended from perception to all judgements whatever. In every case of every sort of judgement, the man himself is the measure of what he judges, and what seems so to him is so to him. No one ever thinks falsely.

Socrates is made to controvert this position and maintain that error does occur. What means does he use for doing this?

It is quite obvious to anybody, when he is not bemused with words, that error does occur; and therefore one way of refuting an argument that error does not occur is to call to mind various situations in which we are all quite convinced that there is a difference between erroneous and correct thinking. And this is one of the ways that Socrates is made to use. For example, he brings us to our senses by asking whether a layman's opinion on whether he is going to have a fever is always just as true as his physician's.

Such methods are good to use on anyone who has allowed his reflections to ruin his common sense; and something very like them, I suppose, has been used very valuably by the Socrates of the twentieth century, Professor G. E. Moore. But they do nothing whatever to explain how a man gets into the absurd position of maintaining that there is no error, or to help the philosopher who, while he knows that error does occur, nevertheless thinks there are some puzzling arguments to the conclusion that it does not occur. It has happened to many philosophers to seem to see that an experienced truth is an *a priori* falsehood. While they experience the fact that error occurs, they seem to see *a priori* proof that error cannot occur. Does Plato bring forward any help for men in this position?

He makes Socrates point out (*Tht.* 170–2) that the doctrine that all opinions are true leads to intolerable trouble if we add to it the thesis that some opinions are to the effect that some other opinions are false. Since all opinions are true, Mr. A's opinion is true; and if Mr. A's opinion is that Mr. B's opinion is false, it follows that Mr. B's opinion is false; but this is impossible by the major premiss that all opinions are true. The believer that all opinions are true must therefore deny that there ever has occurred, or ever will occur, an opinion to the effect that some other opinion is false. The statement that all opinions are true implicitly denies the possibility of contradiction. For contradictory opinions are opinions each implying the other's falsehood, and so, if there is a pair of contradictory opinions, some opinions are not true.

This is a most valuable argument, but it still has the defect of not showing what is wrong with the considerations that lead people to maintain that all opinions are true. It

shows very forcibly that a man who holds this view is in a
morass, but it does not show the road that took him there or
why he went that way. We may still ask whether Socrates is
made to analyse the arguments that lead to the morass so as to
deprive them of their power to puzzle us in the future.

The answer appears to be no, as far as concerns the first
part of the *Theaetetus*, i.e. the discussion of the thesis that
knowledge is sense. There is no exposure of such arguments
here; and it would have been out of place, because no such
arguments are stated in this part or at least stated at any
length. The general doctrine that error cannot occur is not
argued as such here. What is argued is the particular doctrine
that error cannot occur in sensation, and this is extended into
the doctrine that no error of any sort can occur without any
further argument. The extension is made in a not fully
conscious way, for the speakers fail to distinguish clearly
between the special and the general doctrine. Their failure is
partly caused, probably, by the ambiguity of the words
'φαινόμενον' and 'δοκοῦν', which may mean either sensation
in particular or belief in general.

The situation is different when we turn to the second part
of the *Theaetetus*, which is ostensibly a discussion of the thesis
that knowledge is true opinion, but actually mainly a discussion of error. Here we have two explicit arguments that
error in general is impossible, first that we either know or do
not know each thing, and in neither case can we make a
mistake about it (*Tht.* 187–8), and second that error would be
thinking what is not, but you cannot do that any more than
you can see but not see anything (*Tht.* 188–9).

When these two arguments have been developed, Socrates
does not proceed to point out what is wrong with them.
There must be something wrong with them, for error does
occur; and it is in fact possible to give accounts of them
which will cause a man to cease being puzzled or impressed
by them. Thus we may say that the first argument works by

means of confusing acquaintance with descriptive knowledge, since the word '$\epsilon\iota\delta\epsilon\nu\alpha\iota$' can mean each of these. We must be either acquainted or not acquainted with Theaetetus, but in either case we can believe false statements about him, as that he is now in Thebes. And, as everyone thinks this, there is no plausibility in the argument's premiss once the two senses of '$\epsilon\iota\delta\epsilon\nu\alpha\iota$' have been distinguished.

The second argument works by a false analogy between believing and seeing. The phrase 'I saw Theaetetus' implies that Theaetetus was really there. If he was not there you did not see him but only thought you saw him. That is how we use the verbs of perceiving. We do not speak of 'seeing falsely' and 'seeing truly', but of 'seeming to see' and 'seeing'. And so it is absurd to say 'I saw him but he was not there'. If we used such verbs as 'think' and 'believe' in the same way, it would be absurd to say 'I believed it but it was not so'; and Socrates manages to make this seem absurd by arranging a persuasive analogy between seeing and believing. In fact, however, believing is not analogous to seeing, because in saying 'I believed p' we do not imply anything about the truthvalue of p.

These considerations appear to me to be the best replies to the two explicit arguments which Socrates develops for the thesis that error cannot occur, because they deprive the two arguments of all power to persuade us any more. What Socrates actually proceeds to do, however, seems to be something different and a tactical mistake. Instead of demolishing the arguments, thus restoring the *status quo*, and leaving it at that, which is the only safe thing to do with all arguments leading to absurd conclusions, he seems to embark on positive theories to 'explain' error. There are three of them, first the theory that false opinion is 'allodoxy', second the waxen tablet, and third the aviary. According to the 'allodoxy' theory, false opinion is mistakenly taking one real thing for another real thing. On the waxen-tablet theory, it is hard to say what in unmetaphorical language Socrates is saying. The only literal description of the view that I find is the phrase 'διανοίας πρὸς αἴσθησιν παραλλαγή' (*Tht.* 196C5). The new Liddell and Scott says this means an '*interchange* of intellect and sense, putting one for the other'; but that will not fit Plato's metaphorical descriptions, which seem to demand some such translation as 'a false co-ordination of thought and sense'. The third solution is again expressed in an image, this time of an aviary; and again it is hard to state the theory unmetaphorically. It seems to be that false opinion is 'τῶν ἐπιστημῶν μεταλλαγή' (*Tht.* 199 C10), 'the interchange of knowings', a baffling phrase.

Socrates finds all three solutions inadequate, and is left with the problem of error unsolved. They are indeed inadequate, for the proper solution of the problem of error is merely the exposure of any argument which claims to show that error is impossible. But Socrates' reasons for rejecting them are hardly more adequate. The best of them is the refutation of the waxen tablet by citing the fact that a man may add five to seven and make the answer eleven; for this generalizes the problem and corrects the speakers' tendency to confine their attention to errors connected with sensation, as if that were the sole domain of error. The refutation of the 'allodoxy' solution rests on the definition of thinking as the speech that the soul goes through herself by herself (*Tht.* 189E). 'Think', says Socrates, 'whether you ever tried to persuade yourself that one thing actually is another; on the contrary, is it not the fact that you have never even in sleep dared to tell yourself that after all odd is really even, or anything of the sort?' (*Tht.* 190B). Unfortunately this refutation is fallacious. As Cornford neatly said, it equates 'the act of "mistaking" one thing for another with making the silent *statement* that one thing is the other.'[1] Very likely no one has ever said to himself that Mr. Spaak *is* Mr. Churchill;

[1] Cornford, p. 118.

but for all that Mr. Spaak has often been *mistaken for* Mr. Churchill. Socrates confuses thinking that the sum of these numbers is eleven (when it is really twelve) with thinking that eleven is twelve (196B5 *et al.*). We never do explicitly entertain and believe the statement that 'eleven is identical with twelve'; but we often believe some sum or other to be eleven when in fact it is twelve. The fallacy is cunning because our common way of describing someone else's mistake, when we know it to be a mistake, is very close to the language we should use to describe a certain absurd statement which no one would believe. We may describe a certain mistake by saying 'He thought that Spaak was Churchill', and this is very close to 'He thinks that—quotation mark – Spaak is Churchill—quotation mark.'

Plato tended to think of all error as of the type of believing a person seen in the distance to be Theaetetus when he is not, of mistaking one particular for another particular; and when he faced the fact of purely intellectual error, like summing five plus seven to eleven, he tended to assimilate it to the former type by regarding it as a case of mistaking one particular object of mental seeing, namely twelve, for another particular object of mental seeing, namely eleven. Cook Wilson also tended to think of error as mistaking Theodorus for Theaetetus; and he probably got the tendency from Plato's dialogue.[1] But error is just believing a false proposition; and the false proposition may be of any type whatever, though no doubt there are some types which we are less prone to believe than others, e.g., very simple self-contradictions like 'x is not x'.

The refutation of the aviary is the poorest of the three. It seems to consist in essence of just one short and unintelligible paragraph (199D), after which the speakers go on to play with the absurd idea that the aviary contains 'unknowledges' as well as 'knowledges'. I agree with Cornford that the

---

[1] *Statement and Inference*, I, 109 ff.

refutation is probably fallacious. And I think Lee does so too; at least he controverts Hackforth's argument that it is not fallacious.[1] But of the nature of the fallacy involved I will now give an account somewhat different from Cornford's.

I believe that underlying Plato's whole discussion of error in the *Theaetetus* there is one mistake which is more fundamental than any other he may make here and which is the cause of the speakers' making those other mistakes which I have already pointed out. It is the mistake of assuming that thinking is sensing without organs. Although the company reject the doctrine that knowledge is sense, they do not thereby free their minds from the unconscious assumption that thinking is after all a kind of sensing without organs, a kind of touching with spirit hands, a kind of 'extrasensory perception'!

It is this assumption, I suggest, that makes error a problem to them in the first place. If your hand has grasped an apple, it has grasped it and the apple is necessarily there. It is absurd to say 'He has grasped an apple but there is no apple.' And if thinking is ghostly grasping, it would by analogy be absurd to say that you grasp or 'apprehend' an object but it is not there; and therefore the occurrence of erroneous thoughts is a mystery. Thinking is a kind of sensation and sensation is infallible; therefore error is impossible.

The metaphor of '*ἐφάπτεσθαι*' is used by Theaetetus (190D9). The waxen tablet is a theory that a thought is a result of an object's *touching* the mind as a stylus touches a tablet. The aviary is a theory that the actualization of knowledge is a process of *grasping* as a man grasps a bird in an aviary. The metaphor recurs in Aristotle: 'With regard to incomposites, . . . contact and assertion are truth, . . . and ignorance is non-contact; for it is not possible to be in *error* regarding the question what a thing is, save in an accidental

---

[1] *Classical Quarterly*, 1938, p. 27; 1939, p. 208.

sense; and the same holds good regarding non-composite substances (for it is not possible to be in error about them).'[1]

When Socrates in the *Theaetetus* brings forward the definition of thinking as the speech that the soul goes through herself by herself, the point of it seems to be that in thinking the soul is in her own chamber with her objects about her. She has her objects before her; so how can she make a mistake about them?

I believe that this is the thought behind the brief and puzzling refutation of the aviary theory (at 199D), which gives that refutation whatever plausibility Plato thought it had. If there was anything more to it, in Plato's mind, than just the verbal point which it seems to be, namely 'How can the possession of knowledge make you ignorant?' I think it was this, that thinking is mental touching, like a man grasping a bird, and if you touch a thing it is there.

In the *Sophist*, a somewhat later dialogue, Plato makes another protagonist solve the problem of error to the satisfaction of the company. I have given my description of this solution already in controverting Cornford's view that the Forms are involved in it.

The *Sophist*'s discussion of error seems to differ importantly from that in the *Theaetetus* with regard to the distinction between false belief and false statement. It is one thing to ask how false statement is possible and another thing to ask how false belief is possible, in other words how a false statement can gain anybody's credence. The *Theaetetus* clearly asks the latter question rather than the former. It rarely if ever suggests that it is impossible to construct a false statement; what it suggests is that it is impossible for anyone to believe a false statement when constructed.

In the *Sophist*, on the other hand, the problem of false belief seems to be taken very lightly. Of course false belief is

---

[1] Arist. *Metaph.* θ 10 (on truth), 1051b25, Ross tr.

possible if false statement is possible, for thought is just inner statement (διάνοια μὲν καὶ λόγος ταὐτόν, *Soph.* 263E); it takes the company only a short page to become certain of that (*Soph.* 263D–264B). But the point that bothers them now, the point they take time and pains to establish (*Soph.* 261D–263D), is that false statement is possible. A false statement is discovered to be possible, although each word in it must refer to something real, because statement is necessarily complex, and therefore may assert realities to be combined otherwise than as they are in fact combined.

In view of this, the *Sophist*'s discussion of falsehood and error formerly seemed to me wholly disappointing. I said to myself: 'The commentators who say that the *Sophist* solves the problem of error raised in the *Theaetetus* are mistaken, and Plato was mistaken if he himself thought it did so. For the problem of the *Theaetetus* was how a false statement can come to be *believed*; but the *Sophist* is superficial on that point and concentrates on the uninteresting question how a false statement can come to *exist*. We do not need to have that explained to us. It is perfectly obvious that once a language contains the word "not", or any other device for contradicting, you can construct a pair of statements such that at least one of them must be false, such as "Theaetetus is sitting" and "Theaetetus is not sitting". Furthermore, it seems clear on reflection that the possibility of false speech is not due to the complexity of statement, as the Eleatic stranger says it is. For if my only language was a squawk meaning danger, I could make a false statement by squawking when there was no danger. Furthermore, it seems clear on reflection that the individual words need not necessarily refer to things that really exist. In the stranger's example, "Theaetetus is flying", both the objects indicated really occur at certain place-times; but in the sentence, "The soul is a substance", it is probable that neither of the indicated objects ever occurs. The *Cratylus* was right in maintaining that words have a truthvalue as well as statements (*Cra.* 385).'

Such was the nature of my former disappointment at the way in which the *Sophist* handles the problem of error. But now, without withdrawing much of what I have just said, I have come to think that the *Sophist*'s discussion is valuable and, though not pointed straight at the true solution, gives us a useful nudge.

What is the true solution of the problem of error raised in the *Theaetetus*? I have already urged that the correct solution of the problem of error is merely to show what is wrong with any proffered argument for the conclusion that error cannot occur. And I have also urged that the fundamental reason why the occurrence of error is mysterious to the party in the *Theaetetus* is that they assume that thinking is a kind of disembodied touching. It follows from these two views that the true solution of the *Theaetetus*' problem would be to show convincingly that thought is not a kind of disembodied touching; and I now think that the *Sophist* does, in a rather uncertain fashion, put us on the track of this. I formerly complained that the *Sophist* concerned itself mainly with false statement instead of false belief, and cavalierly connected the two by the doctrine that thought is just inner statement. But I now think that the way to free oneself from the *Theaetetus*' difficulties is precisely to reflect on the intimate connection between thought and words and to realize that thought is not touching but symbolizing. Symbols are the essence of thought; and a symbol is a substitute for the object, to be used precisely when you cannot touch the object. Error is possible because symbols can be used falsely and thought is essentially using symbols. That is the outline of the true answer, and it is fairly near to what the *Sophist* says. The development of this outline would consist in part of showing how it lies in the nature of symbols to be capable of falsehood, and the *Sophist* tries to do that, though I still think that it mistakes a sideline for the main road when it picks out the complexity of a statement as the point where the possibility of falsehood enters, and though I cannot say that it explicitly repudiates the idea that thinking is a sort of grasping.

Thought is not prehensile but symbolic. It is a going beyond what one senses at the moment by means of symbols. As such it is always a venture and a risk. I use the symbols, that is, I think, just because I do not feel. The possibility of error is inherent in that. Whereas, if you touch x, x is there; if you symbolize x, x need not be anywhere at all. And this is true of perception as well as of other thought. For perception is using the present sensation as a symbol of something beyond. It is equally but more obviously true of any words I may apply to my present sensation, as if I say 'This tastes sweet to me now'. Whether I apply the word 'sweet' to my present sensation or, without using any words, pour the crystals into the bowl on the basis of my sensation, I am using a symbol and I may be wrong. To avoid all possibility of error I should have to confine myself to passively receiving the unnamed sensation, and I should thereby avoid all possibility of truth also. It is wrong to say that pure sensation is always true or is infallible or anything of that sort. Pure sensation is neither a statement nor a belief and therefore cannot be either false or true. But the mistake appears to have been made by Epicurus and by Aristotle; and Plato in the *Theaetetus* makes Socrates tentatively entertain it (*Tht.* 179C). The sensation you have is the sensation you have, of course. That is a tautology, and hence necessarily true, no matter how peculiar the sensation you have. But the description you give of your sensation, however careful and however sincere, may be erroneous. We are not infallible describers even of our own present sensations. From the time of the *Theaetetus* onwards, confusion and argument have arisen from failing to separate the obvious truth, that the sensation you have is always the sensation you have, from the falsehood that the account you give yourself of your sensation is always true.

A curious little corollary of the above interpretation of the *Sophist* on error is that the definition of thought in the *Sophist* is not really the same as the definition of it in the *Theaetetus*, though it seems to be so. In both places the language tends to be much the same: the logos that the soul goes through herself by herself. But different parts of this phrase operate in the two dialogues. In the *Theaetetus* it is the 'herself by herself' that counts; the soul has her objects before her in her own chamber, how then can she mistake them? The *Theaetetus* does nothing with the other part of the phrase, namely the word 'logos'. (There is one definition of 'δοξάζειν' in the *Theaetetus* that drops 'logos' altogether: 187 A.) In the *Sophist*, on the other hand, it is precisely and only the word 'logos' that counts. Thought can be erroneous precisely because it is a logos and a logos can be false. Thus the tendencies of the definition of thought are opposite in the two dialogues. In the *Theaetetus* it tends to make thought a form of touching; in the *Sophist* it makes thought not touching but believing symbols.

These passages of the *Theaetetus* and the *Sophist* are concerned with the problem of 'explaining' error, or of answering the question: 'How is error possible?' I have been hinting that it is wrong to ask 'How is *x* possible?' no matter what *x* may be, when we know that as a matter of fact *x* does happen, and that we should confine ourselves to detecting the mistake in any argument that may be brought forward to urge that *x* is impossible. But this cannot be universally true; for, after one has seen a baffling conjuring-trick performed, it is evidently sensible to ask how it is possible.

In the case of a conjuring-trick, the question 'How is *x* possible?' means 'Tell me how to produce *x*, which seems impossible but evidently can be done.' This cannot be the meaning in the case of 'How is error possible?'; for no one wants to be told how to make errors, and no one thinks error impossible.

In general, there seem to be four sorts of thing that a proof of possibility may be. To prove that x is possible may be, first, to point out an existing example of x. Secondly, it may be to prove that x is self-consistent, for self-consistency is one kind of possibility. Thirdly, it may be to rebut particular arguments which lead to the conclusion that x is impossible. And lastly, it may consist in pointing to the causes of x and the sort of conditions under which an x will be realized. In the case of error, this will be the enterprise of pointing out those facts about the world which in general cause errors to occur from time to time. This is a perfectly good enterprise, but it falls under the head much less of philosophy than of biology and psychology. The prime condition for the occurrence of error is that there shall be animals which symbolize and infer, which is also, inevitably, the prime condition for the occurrence of truth.

But when we come to give the causes and conditions of some particular error, say of Mr. A's believing on Friday morning that all x's are y, it is to be observed that the causes and conditions will be of the same sort in general, whether this belief is erroneous or correct. In either case, Mr. A is believing this because he has not seen any x's that are not y, or because one of his authorities has told him so, or because he deeply wishes this to be true, or because he deeply fears that this is true, or. . . . And the list could go on indefinitely. The point is that every one of these causes may lead on one occasion to a false belief and on another occasion to a true belief. There is no sort of cause which is specifically a cause of true beliefs, nor is there any sort of cause which is specifically a cause of false beliefs. For whether a belief is true or false does not depend on how the belief was caused to occur, but on whether, once it has occurred, it corresponds to reality or not. Possibly it might be useful to represent this fact by saying that truth and falsehood are non-natural attributes, a non-natural attribute being one that cannot be a cause or an effect. A statement's being true never causes anything, though a man's believing a statement to be true often does so.

4

DR. POPPER'S DEFENCE OF DEMOCRACY

(*First printed in* The Philosophical Review *in 1951*)

I BEG you to study Dr. K. R. Popper's *The Open Society and Its Enemies* (Princeton, N.J., Princeton University Press, 1950; pp. xii, 732), and not to be deterred from a close and sympathetic study of it by certain serious causes of offence which, I admit, it contains. I venture to make this request because I believe that the book contains very valuable ideas for the statement of what we all greatly need and desire to state, namely, the political and moral values for which the free world will fight.

You will find it easier to overcome the distaste which the book's defects invite, if you will read the chapters in the order XIII–XXV, I–XII. In this way you will read first the chapters on Marx, which are nearly untouched by the characteristic defects of the book and are also the most in tune with our present intellectual climate; and you will read last the chapter on Hegel, which is very much the worst in the book. You will not have significantly greater difficulty in understanding Dr. Popper by reading him in this order, especially if you occasionally look at pages 5–11 for an account of what he means by 'historicism'.

Apart from its overriding importance for everybody as a contribution to our political problem, Dr. Popper's book contains in my opinion excellent contributions to political theory, moral theory, logical theory, the philosophy of history, and the history of philosophy; and I recommend it to anyone who specializes in any of these. I recommend it to

Platonists as the freshest and most original treatment of Plato since Burnet's *Greek Philosophy*.

The book consists mainly of critiques of the politics and sociology of Plato and Marx. Heraclitus and Aristotle come in briefly as satellites of Plato. Hegel comes in briefly as a forerunner of Marx. It is fundamentally an examination of two great influences against democracy and an argument that they are mistaken. (Dr. Popper himself, however, rarely regards his book in just this light. He once calls it 'a critical introduction to the philosophy of politics and of history, and an examination of some of the principles of social reconstruction' [p. v]; but much more often he regards it as 'the story of the rise and influences of some important forms of historicism' [pp. 3–4].)

I am too ignorant of Marx to be a reliable judge of Dr. Popper's critique of Marx; and I shall confine myself to other aspects of his book after the present paragraph. I cannot help thinking, however, that this must be a very good critique of Marx. It is free from the grave defect which mars the chapters on Hegel and Plato; and it is full of sentences that seem to me illuminating. Just one example: 'Marx investigated an unrestrained capitalism, and he never dreamt of interventionism. He therefore never investigated the possibility of a systematic interference with the trade cycle, much less did he offer a proof of its impossibility' (p. 369).

Dr. Popper's reports of what Plato said are astonishing. A startling and alarming translation of *Laws* 942, is printed on the wrapper and twice in the book. As Dr. Popper goes on, he produces several other alarming translations from the *Laws* and elsewhere. Again and again the reader is likely to say to himself: 'Surely Plato did not say this; or at least surely Popper has suppressed something else that puts the matter in a better light.'

A very small proportion of Plato's interpreters have been

dispassionate. Most of them have been very favourable to him; and these have tended to sharpen or even distort their translations and interpretations so as to make Plato nearer than he was to their ideal. Jowett, for example, translated '$\epsilon\pi\iota\kappa o\acute{\upsilon}\rho o\iota$' by 'citizens' in *Republic* 464B, and in two other passages wrote 'citizens' where the Greek has no noun but certainly means 'guards' (423E, 451C), thus giving the false impression that Plato intended his education for all the citizens. Dr. Popper, who is one of the few unfavourable interpreters of Plato, tends to sharpen or even distort his translations and interpretations so as to make Plato *farther* than he was from Dr. Popper's ideal. He is no worse in his way than the pro-Plato interpreters are in their way; but he, like them, fails to reach the admirable and rare objectivity of Lindsay and Shorey. I have examined a large number (though not all) of his translations of Plato and statements about what Plato said, more particularly those attributing to Plato something offensive to democrats and humanitarians; and I will list here the more important errors I have found.

Dr. Popper is mistaken in believing (pp. 139, 497) that *Republic* 547A (the 'mystic number') takes back the earlier position that, if a gold or silver child is born to bronze parents, he is to be transferred to the governing class. This passage forbids the mixing of the metals. But the transference of such a child would not be a mixing of the metals. Since the child was of a different metal from his parents, a mixing of the metals would occur if the child remained with them. The prohibition of the mixing of metals, together with the doctrine that silver children are occasionally born of bronze parents, does not prohibit but on the contrary commands the promotion of such a child. Similarly, Dr. Popper is mistaken in thinking that *Republic* 434B–D, forbids such promotion; it forbids a man to do work for which his metal is unsuited. (Popper, pp. 497 and 555. On the latter page '435C' is an error for '434C'.) The most that can truly be said against

Plato on this point is that he provided no machinery by which silver children of bronze parents could be discovered early enough to receive a guardian's education, and that he did not realize that a great deal of talent will always go to waste unless there is a system, such as universal formal education, for testing every child.

Gorgias 488E f. does not say that the view that justice is equality agrees with nature itself; it only argues that this follows from a certain view put forward by Callicles. This is a fairly important mistake because Dr. Popper makes great use of this *Gorgias* passage in imputing dishonesty to Plato (Popper, p. 91).

Republic 368B ff. and 432B ff. are not meant, in my opinion, to lead us to believe that 'Plato omitted none of the more important theories [about justice] known to him'. This also is important for the dishonesty argument (Popper, p. 93).

I think it incorrect to say (p. 48) that in *Republic* 425DE and 427A, Plato forbids his rulers to legislate for the lower classes and for their petty problems. What Plato forbids here is petty legislation, and that is something different.

Socrates in the *Crito* declares his loyalty to 'the laws and the fatherland', not to democracy (Popper, p. 188).

I believe with Taylor that *Laws* 904C10 is nothing about 'level of rank', and I am not at all convinced by Dr. Popper's argument for his translation (pp. 38, 487).

Dr. Popper writes that Plato 'recommended in the *Laws* colonization and birth control and homosexuality . . . as means for keeping the population constant; see *Laws* 740D–741A and 838E'. This statement is false as far as concerns homosexuality. There is no mention of homosexuality in 740D–741A, while 838E is flatly against homosexuality as is the whole of 836–9. To the best of my belief Plato is against homosexuality wherever he mentions it in the *Laws*, having changed his view since his middle period.

Nothing particular depends on this mistake, however (Popper, p. 583).

Timaeus 31A much more probably means 'The resemblance would thus be explained, more precisely, not as to these two things, but as to that superior thing which is their prototype.' (Popper, p. 30).

Republic 485B πλανωμένης ὑπὸ γενέσεως καὶ φθορᾶς was in the English edition 'drift from generation to degeneration', and has now been altered to 'stray towards generation and degeneration' (p. 144), very likely owing to criticism by Mr. J. D. Mabbott, whose help Dr. Popper acknowledges (and to whom I also owe much in this discussion). Dr. Popper's translation is still not good enough, however. Lindsay renders it: 'driven to and fro by generation and decay'.

Dr. Popper does not always grasp Plato's deprecatory and ironical manner of writing. Thus οὐ πάνυ φυλακικοί means 'not altogether fit' rather than 'altogether unfit' (p. 83). Thus too 'It would be dishonest if I were to refuse' is too solemn for Ἀλλὰ μέντοι . . . βούλομαί γε, εἰ μὴ ἀδικῶ (p. 98, translating *Rp.* 430E1). What exactly this phrase means is, I think, not known for certain. Perhaps something like 'I will, or I'm a crook' (material implication). Undoubtedly something lighter than Dr. Popper gives. Even Dr. Popper's conviction that the *Menexenus* is ironical is, I venture to think, a partial failure to grasp the nature of Plato's irony. The *Menexenus* is a baffling mixture of the serious and the ironical, scoffing and love, compounded of his love for Athens and his hate of democracy, which were so intertwined as to baffle Plato himself as well as his readers.

Dr. Popper, like nearly all translators, sometimes renders the meaning more precise or pointed than it was in his text. For example, 'the only true original' (p. 492) is a sharpening of ὀρθῆς μονῆς (*Plts.* 297CD). I could name perhaps a dozen such sharpened passages. This is a fault, since clearly the ideal demands that our translation shall be indeterminate or vague in whatever respects the original is so. But it is a minor fault, since sharpening the meaning is not perverting or concealing it.

In sum, we may say that Dr. Popper's translations of Plato belong in the usual somewhat biased class, and not in the rare objective class of Lindsay and Shorey; but they differ from the usual member of the class in that their bias is the opposite of the usual one.

Biased though they are, they should certainly not be disregarded. They draw attention to real and important features of Plato's thought that are usually overlooked. In particular, Dr. Popper's show piece, the horrible passage from *Laws* 942 about never acting on one's own, is correctly translated. (It might be urged that Plato intended this to apply only to the military life of his citizens, and it is true that the passage begins as a prescription for army discipline; but by the end Plato is clearly wishing to extend it to all life; cf. 'the anarchy must be removed from all the life of all the men' [*Laws* 942D1].) Sound too are the report (p. 140) that the *Laws* proposes to put to death atheists who cannot be 're-educated' (*Laws* X, is distinctly reminiscent of contemporary Communist procedure), and the translation on page 588 of *Laws* 950D–951A. Sound also is the translation of *Statesman* 293C–E on pages 162–3, implying that rulers who know are justified in ruling and killing without due process of law. The translation on page 149 of *Republic* 473D5, as 'suppressed by force' is correct; Plato is saying there that those who are not rulers must be prevented from philosophizing.

The translation 'lordly lie' in *Republic* 414 (Popper, pp. 138, 553) is in my opinion about as accurate as any. I reject Cornford's 'plain fact that ψεῦδος cannot, in this context, mean a "lie", if a lie is a false statement made with intent to deceive' (*The Unwritten Philosophy*, p. 133). To me it seems a plain fact that Socrates is here depicted as intending the citizens of Callipolis to believe something which Socrates knows to be false, namely, that they were born from the earth, and that each of them has mixed into him one and only one of the four metals, gold, silver, iron, bronze.

However, since I do not think that Plato intended to give a cynical impression of himself or his 'Socrates' here, I prefer the translations 'falsehood' and 'fiction' to 'lie'. The word '$\psi\epsilon\hat{v}\delta os$' meant either, since the Greek language did not distinguish the two as clearly as the English does. (Even English does not distinguish them enough, since it is not clear in English whether a man is telling a lie if he says something which he believes to be false but which is in fact true.) My present translation of the sentence is: 'Is there any way by which we could invent one of those useful fictions we were speaking of just now, a single really good one, and get the rulers themselves to believe it if possible, or at any rate the rest of the city?'

Plato's views on lying in the *Republic* are:

1. God never lies (382E).
2. A private citizen ought never to lie (389B–D).
3. A ruler ought to have a passionate desire that he himself may know the truth and not be in a state of error (485CD, 490A–C).
4. A ruler sometimes may and must deceive the private citizens (389B).
5. Socrates, or Plato, or the founder of Callipolis, may and must deceive everybody in Callipolis, if he can (414).

Plato does *not* say or believe in the *Republic*:

6. A ruler must have a passionate desire that *other people* may know the truth and not be deceived.

Interpreters who say that Plato said (6) are mistakenly supposing it to be included in (3) above. The essence of the passage on 'the lie in the soul' (382) is that it is always hateful to be oneself deceived but not always hateful to deceive others.

The general startling effect, therefore, of Dr. Popper's translations is not due to his inaccuracies but to his having adopted a fresh and independent approach to Plato.

It is one thing, however, to be correct in most of one's translations and reports on particular passages, and another to be correct in one's general and summary accounts of the tendencies of the whole. Among Dr. Popper's more general views about Plato's politics are these. Plato held that, since the good state lies in the past, and change is nearly always for the worse, our fundamental political demands must be 'Arrest all political change!' and 'Back to nature!' (p. 86). Plato aims in politics at the good of the state rather than at the good of the individual members of the state. What the good of the state consists in is left very vague (Dr. Popper more or less admits by silence that Plato did not, like many later partisans of the state, find its good in war and conquest); but it tends to be order and stillness and measure and propriety, for Plato had the aesthetic attitude toward politics and regarded the creation of a good constitution as if it were the painting of a beautiful picture (cf. *Rp.* 501). Plato was (and still is) a powerful enemy of democracy, of the open society, of equality, and of freedom.

I agree with Dr. Popper that Plato was an enemy of democracy, of equality, and of freedom, and that he aimed at the good of a superbeing, 'the city as a whole', rather than at the goods of all the citizens. It would perhaps even be true to say that Plato did not aim at the good either of the citizens or of the city, but merely at getting the city into a certain condition which he wanted as such. Plato was like a keen gardener, who would not naturally say that he was aiming either at 'the good of all the flowers' or at 'the good of the garden as a whole', but rather that he was aiming at 'having the most beautiful garden in the county', or 'getting the garden into perfect condition'.

I disagree, however, with Dr. Popper's general account of Plato's politics on two points. First, I think he overdoes Plato's horror of change. I deny that Plato's fundamental poltical demand is 'Arrest all political change!' or 'Back to nature!' Dr. Popper's view here is a consequence of his view that Plato was a 'historicist'. 'Historicism' is one of Dr. Popper's private enemies. I shall later give some account of it and some reason to think that there is not really much of it in Plato.

My other objection to Dr. Popper's general account of Plato's politics is that it omits Plato's most important argument. Dr. Popper does not bring out or face Plato's best and most serious argument for his political proposals, namely that government is a science and science should be left to experts. Plato urges, and Plato sincerely believed, that it is as absurd to govern by popular vote as it would be to conduct medicine or navigation by popular vote. That is the point of the simile of the Ship in *Republic* 488. The error of democracy, according to Plato, is that it denies the possibility of science in government; and his fundamental political demand is not what Dr. Popper says it is but 'Leave government to those who know how!' Plato maintains that some men can know for certain about these matters, and that this knowledge gives them the right to compel the other men for the good of the whole. This is a very important argument, and similar to one regularly put forward by the Roman Catholic church on behalf of a similar claim to the right to compel. The essential point, both of Catholic doctrine and of Plato's politics, is this: the possession of absolute knowledge of good and evil gives the right to compel, and some men do possess some absolute knowledge of good and evil.

A similar claim has sometimes been put forward in the last hundred years by persons calling themselves by some such title as 'political scientist'. I have heard an eminent lady broadcast a talk on politics which ended with an appeal to 'let the scientists have a chance'.

It is not at all easy to meet this argument. The best existing answer known to me is John Stuart Mill's essay, *On Liberty*; but it is not good enough, and urgently needs to be rewritten. In view of the excellent ideas on politics which Dr. Popper's book contains, I think he could have given us a valuable critique of this main argument of Plato's, and it is a thousand pities that he has disregarded it.

Dr. Popper holds that Plato perverted the teaching of Socrates, and only Antisthenes continued it as it really was. To him Plato is a very harmful force in politics but Socrates a very beneficial one. Socrates died for the right to talk freely to the young; but in the *Republic* Plato makes him take up an attitude of condescension and distrust towards them. Socrates died for truth and free speech; but in the *Republic* 'Socrates' advocates lying. Socrates was intellectually modest; but in the *Republic* he is a dogmatist. Socrates was an individualist; but in the *Republic* he is a radical collectivist. And so on.

What is Dr. Popper's evidence for the views of the real Socrates? It is drawn exclusively from Plato himself, from the early dialogues, and primarily from the *Apology*. Thus the angel of light with whom he contrasts the demon Plato is known to us only from the demon's own account! Is this absurd?

It is not absurd, in my opinion, but entirely correct. I too hold that almost all the good evidence for Socrates' views is in the earlier works of Plato, and that from these we can tell that the views of the mature Socrates were immensely different from the views of the mature Plato. The argument for this position has never been more clearly and persuasively set out than it is in Dr. Popper's admirable discussion of the Socratic problem and the Burnet–Taylor theory (pp. 598–

605). The general nature of it is that we can see in the dialogues a steady change from one sort of Socrates to another sort of Socrates, and that the order given to the dialogues by this criterion agrees with the order given by stylometry, and that at or near one end of the series stands the *Apology*, which is the most likely of all the works to be historical because it alone describes a scene which a great many people witnessed and were impressed by. The dialogues cannot all be historical because the order of their dramatic dates would give a most unlikely fluctuation in the opinions of 'Socrates'. In the *Republic*, whose dramatic date is about 421 according to Taylor, Socrates is sure that the soul survives death. In the *Apology*, whose dramatic date is 399, he is quite agnostic on the point. In the *Phaedo*, whose dramatic date is a month later in 399, he is once more sure that the soul survives death and provides elaborate and powerful arguments on the matter.

Dr. Popper's attitude towards the pair, Socrates and Plato, is curiously parallel to, though on a much larger scale than, his attitude towards the pair, Pericles and Thucydides. Here again Dr. Popper considers the one, Pericles, a very good man and the other, Thucydides, a bad man; and here again his whole evidence for the goodness of the good one is drawn from the writings of the bad one! The fact that each of his villains so well understood the aims and ideals of one of his heroes is good evidence that the villains were less villainous than he thinks.

I pass now from the question how accurately Dr. Popper reports what Plato actually said and intended in politics, to the question what judgement should be passed on Plato's views in politics. Are Dr. Popper's criticisms of Plato's politics to be accepted?

Dr. Popper's judgements of the value of Plato's politics are as follows. As a sociologist Plato said many shrewd and illuminating things about society, notably in *Republic* VIII;

but as a political guide he is not to be followed, either by his own criterion or by ours. He is not to be followed by his own criterion because it is too vague to indicate any line of action in particular and too vague to justify any of the miseries which all governmental action necessarily produces. For Plato's ultimate criterion is the Form of the Good, and this remains empty and unknown, both in the *Republic* and apparently also in the lectures on the Good. In practice Plato never justifies any of his actual political proposals by an appeal to the Form of the Good, but tends rather to justify each one by its own appeal to certain common values, among which those of aesthetic order and political subordination are prominent.

Plato's proposals cannot be justified by our criterion, for our criterion of political action (or at least the one that Dr. Popper urges us to adopt) is the diminution of human misery, and Plato's practical proposals would have the opposite effect. This is mainly because the only way to secure the goods which government is able to secure for man, without at the same time suffering the great evils which government is liable to inflict on man, is to ensure that the rulers are checked and controlled to some extent by the whole population, made responsible to the population, made to lose their power automatically after a few years; whereas Plato's chief practical proposal, urged over and over again, is that the rulers shall be absolutely irresponsible and untrammelled and perpetual. 'The right of the people to judge and to dismiss their government is the only known device by which we can try to protect ourselves against the misuse of political power' (p. 316). We cannot do it by inventing institutions guaranteed to produce a perfect ruler every time, because there cannot be such institutions. 'It appears to me madness to base all our political efforts upon the faint hope that we shall be successful in obtaining excellent, or even competent, rulers' (p. 121). Replace Plato's 'question: Who should rule? by the new question: How can we so organize political institutions that bad or incompetent rulers can be prevented from doing too much damage?' (p. 120).

That is Dr. Popper's main judgement on Plato's politics. I will mention also two of his less important, but still very important, judgements. First, the reasons which Plato offers us for adopting his definition of justice are, though showy in presentation, extremely feeble in logic (namely *Republic* IV, 432–44, esp. 442–4). Second, Plato fails to fails to distinguish between the man who acts for the good of the state and the man who acts for the good of his fellow citizens, and therefore assumes that the good man is he who is devoted to the good of that superbeing, 'the city as a whole', and is prepared to hurt or kill any or all of his fellow citizens for the sake of 'the city as a whole'.

These judgements on Plato's political proposals seem to me true and very important. I am inclined to extend the last of them by adding that no man, once he has clearly grasped the distinction between the good of all his fellow individuals, and the good of some other, unseen superbeing called 'the city' or 'the state' or 'the nation' or 'Germany', will ever prefer the good of that superbeing to the good of all his fellows. (I do not mean that he will necessarily deny the existence of that superbeing. Dr. Popper does not deny it, for he urges us to treat the aggressor state harshly but its citizens lightly [p. 576]. I do not deny it either, for I want to say such things as 'all states are criminals', by which I do not mean that all or most of the citizens of most states are criminals.)

I wish briefly to defend these judgements of Dr. Popper's against two very common arguments. The first of these is the argument which goes: 'But Plato explicitly tells us that in his ideal city everything and everyone is to be happy and good, and the perfection of the rulers is to be assured. Hence it is thoroughly perverse and bad of you to suggest that he

doesn't.' The other is the argument that 'we must judge
Plato by the standards of his own time, not by those of ours'.

If a man says in magnificent language 'O let us all be happy
and good', if he paints a utopia in eulogistic terms with very
great artistic beauty, many readers cannot believe that the
means which he proposes for realizing his utopia could
possibly lead in fact to horrible consequences; and to every
attempt, by Grote or Popper or any other commentator, to
point out the dreadful effects that Plato's proposals would in
fact have, these bewitched readers only reply: 'But Plato *says*
that he intends everything to be lovely and good.' How often
have I read in the papers of examinees some such statement as
'In Plato's state the rulers are to be perfect men' put forward
as if it answered all objections and solved all political problems. But anyone who feels inclined to make that remark
surely ought to turn his attention to the question: 'Is it
likely that the practical proposals which Plato makes would
have the lovely results he says they would have?' In order to
answer this question one has to determine first what Plato's
practical proposals are. This is roughly the question what is
left when we disregard his evaluative language. 'Let the
rulers be happy and divine men' (cf. *Rp.* 540C2) is not a
practical proposal because 'divine' is an evaluative word
here. We need to know the practical non-evaluative steps by
which Plato thinks that a result to which he would apply this
evaluation could be brought about. Now one of these
proposals is that the rulers shall always be chosen by the
existing rulers and never elected by the people; the government is to perpetuate itself instead of being chosen by the
people every few years. This having been ascertained, the
next question is: 'What is the evidence as to whether this
device, the self-perpetuation of the government, does in fact
tend on the whole to produce governors who are "happy and
divine" more than the device of democracy?' Then, of course,
the answer is that the *Republic* contains no discussion of the

evidence, and that the evidence is in fact the other way.

'Plato has made quite sure that his rulers shall be first-class persons.' What a wonderful muddle that is! In what sense does writing a book make sure of anything you say in the book? How has Plato achieved this splendid feat? Did he do it by just writing the sentence 'Our rulers shall be first-class persons'? Or did he do it by writing this sentence many times over, in different forms, until his readers were confused into believing it? Or did he do it by mentioning certain arrangements and saying or implying both that these arrangements were possible and that, if they were carried out, then by the laws of nature it would certainly follow that first-class rulers appeared? And if so what are these laws of nature and how has Plato proved their truth?

In answer to the argument that 'we must judge Plato by the standards of his own time' I suggest that it is impossible for anyone to judge anyone except by his own actual standards. You cannot judge Plato except by your own standards. You can, of course, inquire how Plato's contemporaries judged him; but that is not judgement but history. And supposing there is a doctrine which I believe to be deadly at all times, and this doctrine is impressively recommended by an ancient thinker; am I to refrain from saying, as impressively as I can, that his doctrine is deadly? Obviously not.

But it is one thing to urge that a thinker's doctrine is deadly, and another thing to pour blame and abuse upon him for having taught it, and impute to him bad motives for teaching it. And here, alas, I come to the grave defect of Dr. Popper's book, which takes so much from its greatness and will so sadly diminish its influence. He is not content to point out the dangerous nature of Plato's doctrine; he must also condemn Plato as a criminal and speculatively attribute the worst causes and motives to his doctrines.

The historicist's overemphasis on change is 'a symptom of an effort needed to overcome his unconscious resistance to the idea of change' (p. 16). The motive of those who announce historicist views is 'to support the revolt against civilization' (p. 6). The *Republic* fairly generally adopts the method 'of making some concession to the reader's sentiments . . . before the main attack upon humanitarian ideas is launched' (p. 501). Plato's 'attack upon equalitarianism was not an honest attack. Plato did not dare to face the enemy openly' (p. 92). 'I do not see how Plato's method of impressing upon his readers the belief that all important theories have been examined can be reconciled with the standards of intellectual honesty' (p. 93). 'One is tempted to think that Plato knew its weakness, and how to hide it' (p. 99). 'Guileless people have persuaded themselves of the humaneness of Plato's intentions' (p. 103). Yet 'I wish to make it clear that I believe in the sincerity of Plato's totalitarianism' (p. 107). 'Whether we witness in Plato's writings a cynical and conscious attempt to employ the moral sentiments of the new humanitarianism for his own purposes, or whether we witness rather a tragic attempt to persuade his own better consciousness of the evils of individualism, we shall never know. My personal impression is that the latter is the case, and that this inner conflict is the main secret of Plato's fascination' (p. 108). 'The fundamental sincerity of his belief that there is an urgent need to arrest all change can, I think, hardly be questioned' (p. 141). 'I am ready to grant his fundamental benevolence' (p. 166). (But 564–6 is an argument that Plato was not a humanitarian.) 'He felt . . . that he was betraying Socrates' (p. 191). 'I cannot doubt the fact of Plato's betrayal [of Socrates]' (p. 190).

'Plato's philosophical education has a definite political function. It puts a mark on the rulers, and it establishes a barrier between the rulers and the ruled' (p. 145). This is finding subconscious motives for Plato's proposals and is untestable. Plato says that the rulers must learn philosophy because ruling can be a science and philosophy is the way to science. Dr. Popper should have examined this rational and explicit argument instead of making an untestable imputation.

I feel no doubt about Plato's good intentions. Has Dr. Popper never had the depressing thought that perhaps some important truths are too subtle or strange ever to be accepted by the majority of men, and that the contradictories of these truths, important and dangerous falsehoods, will always convince the majority of men whenever they are brought forward? If this horrible state of affairs should be actual (and there is nothing in logic to prevent its being so), what would be the best tactics for one who wished to make happiness prevail? One must answer: The tactics exhibited by Plato in the *Republic* in combating equalitarianism, which he may well have believed to be a dangerous falsehood which will always strike the majority as a truth. I am not on Plato's side; but I am not prepared to blame him for what I think may have been an honest dilemma. If Plato deliberately kept quiet about the equalitarian view of justice, he did it with good intentions towards men, just as many people today think that you must keep drugs and the knowledge of drugs from men for their own good.

Plato did not deliberately confuse the 'protectionist' policy for the state with selfishness in order to persuade his readers that the protection policy is identical with the cynical selfishness of Thrasymachus (p. 117). He honestly failed to distinguish them and was himself in the confused state which Dr. Popper says he was cynically trying to bring on others. Dr. Popper's acute and valuable discovery of a confusion in Plato's text is weakened, not strengthened, by his adding that the confusion was deliberately put there by the author in order to deceive the reader.

What does Dr. Popper think was the real purpose of these wicked deceptions which he attributes to Plato? To increase human misery? To establish the reign of Plato's class? To establish the reign of Plato himself? To make a historicist theory come true? Dr. Popper is vague on this point, although he says that the *Republic* is Plato's own bid for political power. But a clear and convincing answer to this question is essential to establishing any claim that Plato's ultimate purpose was cruel or selfish.

As evidence for deliberate deception Dr. Popper says that the equalitarian theory of justice, which the *Republic* omits to mention, was well known to Plato because he had stated it in the *Gorgias*. I have said that Dr. Popper's reading of the *Gorgias* is not quite accurate on this point in my opinion; but that does not settle the matter. Dr. Popper could say that the early dialogues with their picture of Socrates develop a fairly full humanitarian theory, which therefore must have been well known to Plato when he wrote the illiberal middle and late dialogues; therefore he must have been deliberately suppressing a case in his middle and late periods. Such an argument would be without force, however, for two reasons. First, one is not obliged always to state and refute all one's juvenile opinions that may disagree with one's present assertions. People should be allowed to change their minds without always publicly refuting their earlier opinions; it would often be a bore if they did so. Second, authors are often unaware that their opinions have changed as much as they have, and fail to see in their own works the contradictions which glare at other readers. For my part, I think that Plato never realized how unsocratic he had become, either in politics or in method. I have developed in my *Plato's Earlier Dialectic* the view that he never realized how unsocratic he had become in method (*P.E.D.*, pp. 83–4).

This rage to blame is, I regret to say, still more prominent and repellent in the chapter on Hegel. Schopenhauer's offensive abuse of Hegel had better not have been quoted (pp. 228–9). Ignorant though I am of Hegel, I can hardly believe that Dr. Popper has good evidence that Hegel 'wants to stop rational argument, and with it, scientific and intellectual progress' (p. 235). The horrible sentences which he quotes from Hegel would have been more effective without the imputation that Hegel did not believe them and wrote them for gain. It is disgusting to write 'When Fichte made these remarks [which were very favourable to the French] he was negotiating for a university position in Mainz, a place then controlled by the French' (p. 248).

Dr. Popper shows no sorrow or pity for the meanness and brutality of the mean and brutal. It would be better if he could replace his hatred of mean and brutal men with sorrow and pity for them, and if he could be greatly more cautious in inferring that a man was mean and brutal from the dangerous tendency of his opinions. Let us insist on the deadliness of the doctrine rather than impute bad motives to the man.

If we discover that another man's ultimate moral principle is different from ours, what should we do? If, for example, Dr. Popper's ultimate criterion of morality is the diminution of human misery, but Plato's is the interest of the state (p. 106), what should Dr. Popper do about this? Surely blame and abuse are worse than useless.

In his eagerness to blame, I think Dr. Popper occasionally gets himself into untenable positions. He uses the word 'utilitarian' to blame Plato's moral code (p. 106); but his own code is in my opinion utilitarian too. He uses the *Republic*'s statement that the rulers must sometimes deceive their subjects in order to blame Plato; but he does not confess allegiance to the Kantian principle that the duty of truth-telling is absolute, and he could not do so without contradicting his own doctrine that the duty of minimizing misery is absolute. He holds that Plato did not dare to challenge openly the moral appeal of the forces he tried to break (p. 108); but he himself, as I have said, fails to challenge openly Plato's central argument for his political views. He should have applied further his own excellent doctrine that we should take 'arguments seriously, and at their face value, [instead] of seeing in them nothing but a way in which deeper irrational motives and tendencies express themselves' (p. 436).

There is a minor but also serious obstacle to the appreciation of this book, namely, the mass of 'isms' and Dr. Popper's reluctance to define them. We find essentialism, historicism, social engineering, nominalism, collectivism, tribalism, open society, closed society, democracy, naïve monism, critical dualism, naïve naturalism, naïve conventionalism, biological naturalism, psychological naturalism, positivism, holism, totalitarianism, humanitarianism, equalitarianism, individualism, protectionism, nihilism, personalism, institutionalism, racialism, radicalism, reinforced dogmatism, psychologism, vulgar Marxism, economism, capitalism, activism, interventionism, and historism (which 'must not, of course, be mixed up with historicism', p. 394). In the last paragraph of page 399 there are three different names for the same theory, and it would have been better to omit every one of them. I could point to several other passages from which the 'ismic' words could easily and beneficially be removed. When he writes that 'conservative principles are usually an explosion of ethical nihilism, that is to say, of an extreme moral scepticism, of a distrust of man' (p. 72), surely it would have been in every way better to write 'conservative principles are usually an expression of a distrust of man'.

Dr. Popper writes that his book, 'dealing as it does with philosophical positions, . . . can hardly avoid, for the sake of brevity, introducing *names* for these positions. This is the reason why I have to make use of so many "isms". But in many cases these names are introduced only after the positions in question have been described' (p. 625). I think, on the contrary, that Dr. Popper would have been more intelligible if his book had contained only half as many occurrences of these vague terms, and a good many more pointers to the meaning of those which remained. Many of

them are not defined at all, for Dr. Popper is rather contemptuous of definition. It is, he says, a 'prejudice that
language can be made more precise by the use of definitions'
(p. 214). 'The precision of a language depends . . . upon the
fact that it takes care not to burden its terms with the task of
being precise' (p. 216). There is truth in this; but it is also
true that the comprehensibility of a book depends on the
reader's knowing or being able to find out what its words
mean. I still do not know what he (or anybody else) means by
'totalitarianism'. The best guess I can make is that he means
the whole political character of Hitler's Germany; but, if so,
I see no sense in the statement that Plato's political programme 'can . . . be fairly described as totalitarian' (p. 87).

Even when these terms are defined, anyone who forgets the
definition is unlikely to be able to find it again, for there is no
index of anything but proper names. The word 'historism' is
defined on page 394; but most readers will have forgotten the
definition by the time they reach page 440, where the word is
used a lot; and Dr. Popper has provided no way for them to
find it again.

The fact that there is no index except of proper names is a
great pity for another reason also. The absence of an index
of the passages discussed in Plato and other authors will
cause this book to have less influence on the study of the
texts than it deserves. What Platonist, for example, interested
in the doctrine of the elementary triangles in the *Timaeus*,
would think it reasonable to look through this big political
volume on the chance that Dr. Popper has dealt with the
passage? But, if there had been an index of passages discussed,
the specialist would have taken the little time required to
consult it and would have discovered that Dr. Popper has a
valuable account of this matter (pp. 527–31). Again, though
it is known that Dr. Popper is an important logician, one
would hardly think it worth while to leaf through this volume
in the hope of finding a contribution to the theory of para-

doxes; yet there is one (pp. 708–12). If there were an index of subjects it could easily be discovered.

I have not undertaken a comparison of this edition with the original English edition of 1945; but it is obvious that on the one hand the outline of the book remains the same, and on the other hand Dr. Popper has made minor changes in the writing, and additions of paragraph length and occasionally of page length.

As to the part of the publishers and printers, the wretched illogicality of putting the period before the quote even when the period is not quoted, so offensive to all logicians, appears to have its grip well round the neck of the Princeton University Press as of most publishers and printers; but they have have allowed Dr. Popper to make a gentle protest (p. 467). I noticed only twenty-three misprints, including 'Eutyphro' three times on page 608. 'Rationalist' is probably a misprint for 'nationalist' on page 247; but the passage is not in the English edition. The book is strong, and easy to read in spite of a long line.

Though Dr. Popper's work seems to me essentially a defence of democracy against two of its most powerful opponents, he regards it mainly as a critique of 'historicism'. By this word he means any theory according to which human history exhibits a necessary and predictable course, a 'destiny' or 'design', any belief that one has 'discovered laws of history which enable [one] to prophesy the course of historical events' (p. 5), with the consequent habit of historical prophecy, and the consequent doctrine that the social sciences, if they are to be of any use, must be prophetic. He discusses such views in several persons, primarily Marx of course, but also Hegel and Toynbee and—rather unconvincingly—Plato. Plato, he says, shrinks back from the last consequences of historicism (p. 24). I should rather say that Plato did not believe historicism at all and did not think that *Republic* VIII, stated an inevitable historical progress. Historicism, I am inclined to think, is always a consequence of belief in either an omnipotent Providence or an omnipresent natural law; and Plato had not thought of either.

As you would expect from the insight into the nature of science which Dr. Popper's earlier book displayed, he offers a most penetrating critique of historicism, and in my opinion he demolishes it. His distinction between historical prophecy and scientific prediction is excellent (p. 540). But he does not make it very clear what the relation of this is to the great topic of democracy or authority which is undeniably his second if not his first theme. He evidently thinks that historicism naturally leads to antidemocratic views. I cannot say with confidence just why he thinks this; but perhaps he holds that the democratic position contradicts historicism because it implies that we can take our political fate into our own hands and make it what we choose. Perhaps, on the other hand, he merely thinks that the future which all historicists so far have predicted has been in fact, though it need not have been, an undemocratic one. Perhaps, thirdly, it is connected with his view that historicists tend to hold that right is future might; what will happen is right merely because it will happen. This doctrine is implied by the phrase 'the verdict of history', whose unsoundness Dr. Popper well shows (p. 439 and elsewhere).

Another of his enemies is 'essentialism', by which he means the habit of looking for essences and of asking questions of the form 'What is the essence of x?' or 'What is the nature of x?' or just 'What is x?' His objection to definition is largely based on the fact that the answer to a 'What is x?' question is a definition of a sort. He recommends that we should search for processes instead of essences, for laws instead of natures, and should ask 'How does light move?' rather than 'What *is* light?'

Dr. Popper seems to say that essentialism and historicism entail each other. On the one hand, historicism needs essentialism (he says [p. 485] that he has shown this in his 'Poverty of Historicism' in *Economica*, 1944–5). On the other hand, Aristotle's essentialism directly leads to three historicist doctrines (p. 205).

I sympathize very much with Dr. Popper's rejection of essentialism. It is indeed the same as my critique of the 'What is *x*?' question both in my *Plato's Earlier Dialectic* and in my *Definition*. I cannot agree with him, however, in thinking that it follows that definition is practically useless or in thinking that there are any very strong connections between essentialism and historicism.

I end by reporting some of Dr. Popper's ethical and political beliefs and proposals which have not clearly appeared in the previous discussion. Natural laws are distinct from normative laws, the latter being norms or demands and not strictly true or false. Norms were not in the first place consciously introduced by man; but they are man-made in that there is no one to blame for them but ourselves. It is our business to improve them as much as we can, if we find them objectionable. Facts and decisions are distinct. Decisions can never be derived from facts, although they pertain to facts. Arguments cannot determine a fundamental moral decision. Nevertheless, they can help it. 'Whenever we are faced with a moral decision of a more abstract kind, it is most helpful to analyse carefully the consequences which are likely to result from the alternatives between which we have to choose' (p. 418). For only so can we really know what our decision is about. Choose therefore to follow reason and experience in the sense of working out the consequences, and of respecting arguments and the other man's point of view. Reason and not love should be the ruler; for we can love only those whom we know, and 'the appeal even to our best emotions . . . can only tend to divide mankind into different categories' (p. 420). The ultimate moral formula is 'Minimize suffering!' not 'Maximize happiness!' 'Of all political ideals, that of making the people happy is perhaps the most dangerous one' (p. 422). All moral urgency has its basis in the urgency of suffering.

Individuals should not worship a state, because the morality of states tends to be considerably lower than the morality of the average citizen. The state should aim at the protection of the freedom of individuals, all the freedom they can have without harming other individuals. Tolerate all those who are not intolerant and do not propagate intolerance. We have the right not to tolerate the intolerant. Both physical and economic freedom defeat themselves if unlimited and must therefore be limited. Democracy, the right of the people to judge and dismiss their government, is the only known device by which we can try to protect ourselves against the misuse of political power. And since political power can control economic power, political democracy is also the only means for the control of economic power by the ruled. 'Only freedom can make security secure' (p. 320). The use of violence is justified only under a tyranny which makes reforms without violence impossible, and should have only one aim, that is, to bring about a state of affairs which makes reforms possible without violence.

Justice is not what Plato said it was, but equal distribution of the burdens and advantages of citizenship and equal treatment of all citizens by equal laws impartially enforced. Whenever possible, let intervention consist not in giving discretionary powers to an officer but in designing a legal framework of institutions. Rely on institutions rather than on the benevolence of persons in power. All politics consists in choosing the lesser evil. Fight existing evils rather than try to establish an ideal good. The attempt to make heaven on earth invariably produces hell.

I am afraid that some may find these principles and demands of Dr. Popper rather trite. They are, I agree, rather obvious. Many of them have been held by most liberals. There is not much that is subtle or obscure in them. Nevertheless, I confess I think Dr. Popper's statement of them very valuable. There are few if any good statements of these doctrines. Obvious political doctrines have been invisible to many intellectuals in the last two decades. Intellectuals, who alone can state these matters rightly, rarely do so because of their tendency to try to be subtle and novel. And there is a quite novel freedom from logical difficulties in the way in which Dr. Popper expresses liberalism.

Postscript. Later editions of this book have added the index of subjects desiderated above, but not the index of passages discussed.

5

THE THEORY OF NAMES IN
PLATO'S *CRATYLUS*

(*First printed in* Revue Internationale de Philosophie *in 1955*)

PLATO'S *Cratylus* is about ὀνόματα, but what are ὀνόματα?
No English word is equivalent to the Greek word 'ὀνόματα',
but nearest to it comes 'names'. We may therefore say
roughly that the *Cratylus* is about names. But an ὄνομα
differs from a name in at least two ways.

(1) In English names are primarily proper names like
'Socrates', and to call 'man' a general name is a little peculiar,
though it is done and the dictionary recognizes it; but in
Greek 'man' is every bit as good an ὄνομα as 'Socrates'.

(2) '"Ονομα' is much closer to 'word' than 'name' is. This
is partly because 'ὄνομα' embraces general nouns far more
easily than 'name' does, and largely because there is no
equivalent for 'word' in Greek. Approximations to our
notion of a word exist in the word 'ἔπος' (but prose does not
like this word), and in the phrase 'μέρος λέξεως' (but that is a
phrase, not a word, and the μέρη λέξεως that Aristotle lists
1456b20 are not words), and in longer expressions including
Plato's 'τὰ τῆς φωνῆς σημεῖα' (*Soph.* 262D); but equivalents
do not exist. The function of the missing word 'word' is
often performed by 'ὄνομα'. Thus, when Epicurus says 'τὰ
ὀνόματα ἐξ ἀρχῆς μὴ θέσει γενέσθαι' (Diogenes Laertius,
X, 75–6), he means to be talking about words in general. He
is not conscious of confining himself to one kind of word, as
we are when we talk about names.

Owing to this tendency of the word 'ὄνομα' towards the
meaning 'word', ὀνόματα are not equivalent to names. Also
owing to this tendency, people often think it better to

translate 'ὀνόματα' by 'words' and to say that the *Cratylus* is about words. Yet 'ὄνομα' is 'name' rather than 'word', and the Greeks did not realize nearly as much as we do the distinction between the species name and its genus word. A passage like Plato's *Sophist*, 261D–262C, where the word 'ὄνομα' is laboriously used first in a generic and then in a specific sense, expresses the rare struggle of a great man towards a distinction which, thanks to him, is now common property. Even Aristotle's definition of 'ὄνομα' (*De Int.* 16a19) does not achieve the generality of our 'word'. When a Greek heard the word 'ὄνομα' he thought first of a proper name, then of general names, occasionally also of adjectives, rarely also of verbs (*De Int.* 16b19), still more rarely of prepositions or conjunctions. In his conception of an ὄνομα there lay undistinguished at least five notions that are distinct now: the proper name, the name, the word, the noun, and the subject of predication.

It is still less prudent to translate 'ὀνόματα' by 'language' and say that the *Cratylus* is about language. This translation would be often wrong and never necessary. It may be right to say that 'Socrates' in *Cratylus*, 424–5, is speaking of a plan for an ideal language, but it is certainly not right to use the word 'language' in translating 'τὰ ὀνόματα' in the passage.

A language is 'the whole body of words and of methods of combining them used by a nation, people, or race; a "tongue" ' (*Shorter Oxford English Dictionary*). What, if anything, is the Greek equivalent?

Language is near to φωνή or voice, because it is (in its primary form at any rate) voice articulated as a symbol; and so man's acquirement of language can be referred to as 'φωνὴν καὶ ὀνόματα ταχὺ διηρθρώσατο τῇ τέχνῃ' (Plato, *Prot.* 322A). The word is common in the *Cratylus*, often in its first meaning of 'voice' (e.g. 423B–D), but often also in the meaning of 'language or tongue', as in 'τὴν Ἀττικὴν τὴν παλαιὰν φωνήν', 398D, and 'τὴν Ἑλληνικὴν φωνήν', 409E, and in the third sentence of the dialogue. But it never appears as a subject of investigation in the *Cratylus*, still less as the topic of the dialogue. And Aristotle makes clear in his *Inquiries concerning Animals*, IV, 9, that φωνή is never quite the same as language, because language never is simply what φωνή is primarily, namely, voice produced in a pharynx.

There are three other Greek words that come near to our 'language'. One of these is 'διάλεκτος'. Aristotle (loc. cit.) says that διάλεκτος is the articulation of the voice by the tongue, and is peculiar to man, and varies from man to man. 'Διάλεκτος' comes close to our 'language' in easily bringing up the idea of different dialects or languages; but it departs from it again in suggesting conversation. And conversation is what 'διάλεκτος' means in its few occurrences in Plato, none of which is in the *Cratylus*.

Another Greek word that comes close to our 'language' is 'logos'. Whereas in his *Inquiries concerning Animals* Aristotle finds the peculiarity of man's φωνή to be διάλεκτος, in his *Politics* he finds it to be λόγος (*Pol.* I, 2, 1253a7–18). All beasts, he there says, can signal pleasure and pain by means of voice, but only man with his logos can signal good and bad and their species. Bywater uses the word 'language' to translate 'logos' in Aristotle's *Poetics*, 1456a37 and b7. One can hardly avoid using the word 'language' in translating Plato's 'τὸ τῶν λόγων ἀσθενές' (*Letter* VII, 343A1). And in the *Cratylus* it is possible that 'λόγον' is to be translated by 'language' at 425A.

Nevertheless, logos is not identical with language. 'Two verbs cannot make a language' means something different from 'two verbs cannot make a logos' (see Plato's *Soph.* 262B). A logos can be a statement, which a language cannot be. We can use the word 'logos' to say in Greek that language is man's most valuable possession, but not to say that there are fifty different languages in India. In any case, logos is not the topic of the *Cratylus*; and, when it comes under scrutiny at all in this dialogue, it does so not in its meaning of 'language' but in its meaning of 'statement' (385, 431).

Another Greek word that comes close to our 'language' is 'γλῶττα'. 'Γλῶττα' is indeed in some Greek authors very like our 'language'. In the *Cratylus*, however, so far as I have observed, it always means an organ of the body, the tongue (422E, 423B, 426E, 427A, 427B). Ast cites no use of it in the metaphorical sense from any work by Plato.

Since then neither λόγος nor διάλεκτος nor φωνή nor γλῶττα is the topic of the *Cratylus*, but ὀνόματα, it is usually better to say that the *Cratylus* is about names than to say that it is about language. We may pass the use of 'Sprach-philosophie' and such words in the title of books about the *Cratylus*; but we had better not say that 'the ostensible subject of discussion is the origin of language' (A. E. Taylor, *Plato the Man and his Work*, ed. 2, p. 77), or that 'the main theme of the *Cratylus* is obviously the relation of language to thought and reality' (Shorey, *What Plato Said*, p. 267).

What aspect of names does the *Cratylus* discuss? Their correctness or ὀρθότης. Correctness of names is announced as the topic in the third sentence, and continues to be the sole topic throughout, except that there is something like a short appendix on the theory that all things are always in flux. The *Cratylus* is definitely not one of those dialogues where two apparently unrelated topics seem to share the speakers' attention. It is almost wholly occupied in examining the theory that 'names are not merely random, but have a certain correctness' (397A).

Since the *Cratylus* is solely about the correctness of names, it is not about the origin of names, either wholly or in part. The passage just quoted from Taylor includes, therefore, a second mistake, the common mistake that the *Cratylus* discusses origins. The *Cratylus* discusses two contrary theses, stated at the beginning; and neither of them mentions origins. Plato neither made, nor represented any of his characters as making, the mistake of guessing how language began or supposing he knew how language began. Nobody in the dialogue inquires how names began, or where they began, or when they began, or whether they began more than once, or whether there was a clean breakaway from animal sounds. Plato had as little interest in the origin of names as in other kinds of genesis. (Cf. Julius Deuschle, *Die Platonische Sprachphilosophie*, 1852, S. 44. This is one of the best books on Plato's *Cratylus*.) No argument is brought for or against the proposition that language began as a deliberate and self-conscious invention by some unusually clever man, who proposed it to his companions and had it accepted by them. Otto Apelt, in the introduction to his translation of the dialogue (pp. 2, 4), gives a false impression by using the words 'Ursprung' and 'entstanden'.

The false opinion, that Plato's *Cratylus* discusses the origin of names, is easy to fall into for two reasons. The origin of names was or soon became a common topic with other Greek thinkers; for example, Epicurus discussed it in a passage from which I have quoted a sentence above. And in discussing the origin of names these thinkers used words very similar to the words used by Plato to discuss the correctness of names. Thus the word 'φύσις' is prominent both in Plato's discussion of the correctness of names and in Epicurus' discussion of their origin. This makes it easy to think that Plato is here discussing the origin of names.

Any tendency to think that the *Cratylus* discusses the origin of names is likely to be confirmed by the observation that in this dialogue there are many references to 'the very ancient men who made the names' (411B), to 'the first men in Greece' (397C), and to a certain 'lawgiver' or 'namemaker' (389A1) or 'establisher of names' (389D) or 'onomast' (424A), whose thoughts we are guessing when we try to explain the rightness of a name (e.g. 408B1). It is easy to suppose that this lawgiver is intended to be an historical figure, and from that supposition it would follow that Plato is trying to write history here, trying to describe what happened when men began to talk. And this seems to be further confirmed by all the talk about the debasement of names in the course of time. In making out particular etymologies 'Socrates' frequently supposes that the name as now used is an alteration of the name as first laid down, the alteration being due to time or to a desire for decoration or for euphony (414C).

But this is a misreading of the figure of the lawgiver. He is convenient to Plato because the implausibility of the particular etymologies offered can be palliated by calling our actual names debasements of the work of an original lawgiver. He is convenient because he personifies the idea of the correctness of names, and he does that well because we all easily fall into the error of assuming that the correct form of anything is its earliest form (418E10). He is attractive because he satisfies our desire to find that our culture is due to our own conscious and intentional human thinking working reasonably.

But he is there not as a piece of history but as a mythical device to make it easier to develop an abstract theory. He is introduced (388E1) in a perfectly unhistorical way, as part of an abstract deductive theory, in the present tense not the past tense, and linked with another mythical character, the dialectician (390C). 'Socrates' knows by abstract reasoning on what principle this lawgiver proceeds (389). He is someone who ought to exist if names are to be correct, rather than someone who has existed. In fact, a correct set of names is an ideal to be realized in the future (424BC); and whether our actual names are correct is to be decided after we have ascertained the ideal (425B1–2).

This lawgiver is as much a myth to Plato as the Adam who gave names to creatures is a myth to modernist Christians. He is like the point-particle we imagine in order to work out

Newton's laws of motion. He is like the constructor of the material world in the *Timaeus*, posited in order to explain better the nature of a world that never was constructed because it has always existed. Whenever he is inconvenient, he retires or dissolves. Sometimes he dissolves into a crowd of shadowy lawgivers or namemakers, Greek or barbarian (390A), such as 'those around Orpheus' (400C); sometimes into the human mind (διάνοια, 416B); sometimes into God (397C, 438C). He does not answer the question how names arose but shelves it; and the *Cratylus* has nothing to say on the origin of names.

Max Leky's essay *Plato als Sprachphilosoph* (Paderborn, 1919) is mainly a statement that the topic of the *Cratylus* is the origin of language. 'Die Frage nach dem Sprachursprung bildet ja den Kerninhalt dieses Dialoges' (p. v). He develops this view by taking the discussion of 'first names' as a discussion of the origin of language, and accordingly thinks pages 421–7 the place where Plato gives his own positive line of thought. But by 'first names' Plato does not mean temporally first names but logically first names, that is, names which imitate their nominates directly by their sound or feel, not indirectly by being combinations of first names. A logically first name is not necessarily a temporally first name also. The only necessary connection is that a logically derived name cannot be temporally prior to those particular first names from which it is derived. His 'first names' are the 'elementary' names (στοιχεῖα, 422AB); and his occasional references to the 'oldest' names (421D, 425A, 425E), and to the lawgiver, are merely the usual mythical clothing.

A name is related both to the thing that it means and to the thought or conception that it expresses; but the *Cratylus* deals only with the relation of the name to the thing, and never discusses or even mentions the relation of the name to the thought. It is incorrect to write of 'the question raised in the *Cratylus* concerning the relation of word and conception'

(Felix Heinimann, *Nomos und Physis*, Basel, 1945, p. 51). Aristotle's mistake, that speech symbolizes thought (*De Int.* 16a3), is neither made nor noticed in the *Cratylus*. (Some passages where Plato does mention the relation of names or statements to thoughts are: *Tht.* 189E, 206D; *Soph.* 263E; *Phlb.* 38; *Letter* VII, 342–4.)

The *Cratylus* deals solely with the relation of names to things. It is occupied almost throughout in discussing a certain theory about the relation of names to things, the theory that 'every thing has a right name by nature', ὀνόματος ὀρθότητα εἶναι ἑκάστῳ τῶν ὄντων φύσει πεφυκυῖαν (third sentence of the dialogue), or that 'the names of things belong to them by nature', φύσει τὰ ὀνόματα εἶναι τοῖς πράγμασι (390E). I shall sometimes call this the 'nature-theory of names'. The natural correctness of a name consists, according to the speakers in the *Cratylus*, in its showing the nature of its nominate, 396A. There is one and the same correctness for every name, both first and last, to wit that it should show what each thing is, 422CD, that it should make things plain to us, 422DE.

The task of the name being to show the thing, it will achieve this by imitating the essence of the thing (423). Names should be 'made as much as possible like the things they are to show' (433E). (Like is to be named by like.) 'It makes all the difference in the world whether we show what we show by means of a likeness or by any chance means' (434A). How exactly this likeness is or would be realized the dialogue does not claim to know; but 'Socrates' is made to give what he calls a 'hybristic and ridiculous' sketch, according to which the letters imitate the things they mean by the manner of their production in the mouth (426–7). Speaking involves such acts as shaking the tongue, pressing the tongue, rolling the tongue, making breathy sounds, and stopping the breath. A name will be right so far as these characters of its production resemble the characters of its nominate. That will be the rightness of first names or elements. Then there will be secondary names whose rightness will consist in their being correct combinations of the first names.

The nature-theory as conceived by the speakers entails the following propositions. It entails, first, that it is not always an *accident* (ἀπὸ τοῦ αὐτομάτου, 397A, 420B) that the name of a thing is whatever it is. It entails, secondly, that mere *agreement* does not constitute a name. Οὐ τοῦτο εἶναι ὄνομα ὃ ἄν τινες συνθεμένοι καλεῖν καλῶσι (383A). There is some other rightness of names besides agreement and convention (συνθήκη καὶ ὁμολογία, 384D; cf. 433E, 434E–435C). (Aristotle also implied that the nature-theory entails that mere agreement does not constitute a name, when he wrote that '[A name] is by agreement, because no name exists by nature', *De Int.* 16a27.)

The speakers also hold that the nature-theory entails, thirdly, that mere *custom* does not constitute a name (ἔθει τῶν ἐθισάντων 384D). A certain set of letters may be a customary name of a certain thing in a certain part of the world; but that is irrelevant to the question whether this set of letters is a naturally right name of that thing.

The nature-theory of names entails, fourthly, that the mere *fiat* of a private individual cannot create a genuine name. If the nature-theory is true, it is false that 'whatever anyone says a thing is to be called is a name of that thing' (385A, D). If the nature-theory is true, you cannot make names just as you please; and Protagoras' view that 'man is the measure of all things' is false in the sphere of names at least (386A). 'A sound that I can use *as I please* is not a *word*' (Malcolm, expounding Wittgenstein in *The Philosophical Review*, 1954, October).

We have now four propositions which the nature-theory as conceived by the speakers denies:

1. It is always an accident that the name of a thing is what it is.

2. A name is right if people agree to use it as a name.
3. A name is right if there is a custom of using it as a name.
4. A name is right if anybody posits it as a name.

The speakers all tend to assume that these four are equivalent. In 384D 'Hermogenes' passes from agreement (D1) to individual fiat (D2), and thence to custom (D8), as if he were expressing one and the same theory in three different ways. In 434–5 'Socrates' is only a little more critical on the point; he at first says that custom and agreement do not differ, then admits that they may differ, and then at once goes back to assuming that they do not differ. In truth no two of these propositions are equivalent; for an agreement made between men is different from a custom reigning among men, and each of them is different from a decision made by one man, and all three are different from an accident. Hence the anti-nature theory of names is ill defined in the *Cratylus*.

The nature-theory entails, fifthly, that a name can be *better or worse* as a name. For a name is an imitation of the essence of a thing; and an imitation can be more or less like the thing it imitates. It can be less like it without necessarily becoming wholly unlike it and so ceasing to imitate it at all. And it must be partly unlike it, for if it were exactly like it it would be not an imitation but a replica (432).

About this fifth consequence of the nature-theory the speakers are not all agreed, at first at any rate; for 'Cratylus', although he counts as the champion of the nature-theory, holds at first that a name is either perfectly correct or not a name at all. But 'Socrates' shows him, in a full and careful argument (429A–433C) that he is contradicting himself (433B) in holding both that there is a natural rightness of names and that a name is either perfectly right or not a name at all. (In fact, the statement, that a name is either perfectly correct or not a name at all, is a consequence of the anti-nature doctrine that anything is a name if it is appointed to be a name by custom or by agreement or by individual fiat.)

The nature-theory of names entails, sixthly, that there is an *art* in making names. Anything that can be made better or worse requires an art to guide us in making it better rather than worse. A name can no more be made well without art than a shuttle can. It is in fact an organ just as a shuttle is (389). The artist who possessed this art might be called a 'namemaker' or an 'onomast'; and, as the best critic of a work of art is always the man who has to use it, the best critic of the namemaker's product would be the dialectician, the man who knows how to ask and answer questions (390C).

I turn now to some propositions which the speakers do *not* believe the nature-theory to entail, although some people are sometimes inclined to say it does entail them. In the first place, the speakers do not hold that the theory, that correct names for things exist by nature, entails that correct names are not posited or laid down. They never oppose nature to *positing*, φύσις to θέσις. The word 'θέσις' is not used in the two main denials of the nature-theory, 384D and 435AB. I have noticed it only three times in the dialogue, the three times listed by Ast: 390D, 397C, 401B. In each of these occurrences it means something compatible with φύσις, not opposed thereto. In each of them it means something that happens in any case, whether the nature-theory is false or true. In 390D the thesis or positing of names is a serious matter just because the nature-theory is true. You can posit a name either in accordance with nature, or in accordance with an agreement you have made with other men, or in accordance with nothing but your own choice. The assumption of the speakers is that words have to be posited in any case, whether they are natural or not. The lawgiver posits (τίθεται) the names, that is, he undertakes the θέσις ὀνομάτων, and he tries to do it in accordance with nature. But the mere fact that he posits the names no more decides whether the names are natural than the fact that an ordinary lawgiver posits ordinary laws decides whether those laws are in accordance with nature.

Everything starts by voluntary imposition, according to Plato's usual assumption. His conservatism is not the English idea that the constitution has grown by itself and what has grown naturally is best. It is the Greek conservatism that some great legislator or god has made the natural constitution and we must see that his work is not defaced.

Some interpreters have wrongly assumed that the *Cratylus* does oppose nature to positing, e.g. Proclus (in *Cra.*, ed. Pasquali, p. 4) and Leky (op. cit., p. 84). They may have been led into this error by the fact that Epicurus discussed a certain non-Platonic question about names by means of an opposition between φύσει and θέσει, although Proclus saw that Plato and Epicurus were using the word 'φύσει' in different senses (op. cit., pp. 7–8). Epicurus asked himself the historical question whether the human animal first began to talk as a result of a deliberate establishment (θέσει), or on the contrary without any deliberate act on anyone's part, as so many features of human culture begin (φύσει, Diogenes Laertius, X, 75). Plato on the contrary assumed without reflection that names began through some deliberate establishment, and asked himself whether this establishment was (or could have been) in some way according to nature, or on the contrary would have to be only an arbitrary decision. The resemblance between Epicurus' question and Plato's question is only superficial. (I have learnt much of this from Cyril Bailey's account of Giussani in *The Greek Atomists and Epicurus*, p. 381.) Democritus appears to have come much closer than Epicurus did to the question of the *Cratylus*. He seems, in fact, to have discussed the very same question as the *Cratylus* does by means of taking θέσις or imposition as the contrary of nature or φύσις (Diels, *Vorsokratiker*, Demokritos B 26). Plato in the *Cratylus*, however, never regards the thesis-theory as contrary to the nature-theory.

Secondly, the speakers do not suppose that, in saying that right names exist by nature, they are denying that right names exist by *law*. They do not oppose nature to law, φύσις to νόμος. Nature and law are on the same side in the dialogue. The law is what gives us the natural names of things (388D12); and the lawgiver is the artist who knows what the natural name of a thing is.

Most of the occurrences of 'νομο-' in the *Cratylus* are in the word 'νομοθέτης'. The νομοθέτης or lawgiver, far from being opposed to nature, seeks to follow nature. The word 'νόμος' by itself occurs only six times, so far as I have noticed (384D, 388D, 400E, 401B, 417E, 429B). In 417E it means music. In 400E it merely cites a law or custom about prayer. In 401B it merely appeals to a particular custom. The remaining three occurrences are relevant to the topic of the dialogue.

In 429B 'Socrates' appeals to the fact that laws may be better or worse, to refute 'Cratylus'' view that a name is either correct or not a name at all. 'Cratylus' is the champion of the view that there is a natural correctness of names. But what 'Socrates' is here refuting by referring to law is not 'Cratylus'' main view that there is a natural correctness of names, but his minor view that a name is either correct or not a name. 'Socrates' shows him that his minor view is inconsistent with his main view (433B). Here, then, law is not opposed to nature but on its side. So it is in 388D, for there law and the lawgiver are necessary to give us natural names, since names are tools and require technical skill in the making.

I summarize the above by saying that all occurrences of 'νομοθέτης', and all occurrences of 'νόμος' except one, put νόμος and νομοθέτης on the same side as nature.

There is, however, one occurrence in which νόμος is opposed to nature, and that is its first occurrence, 384D. But even here the word 'νόμος' does not carry the whole weight of expressing the anti-nature theory of names. It is coupled with 'ἔθος', 'usage and custom'. And in the same speech 'Hermogenes' uses still other words to express his theory, συνθήκη καὶ ὁμολογία.

Thus the word '*νόμος*' never serves by itself to express the opponent of the nature-theory. It merely once assists three other words in performing this task. This aberrant use appears only because 'Hermogenes' is scraping up as many different words as he can to express his anti-nature view. In all other parts of the dialogue the anti-nature theory is expressed by other words (*ἔθος, συνθήκη, ὁμολογία*), and '*νόμος*' expresses the nature-theory or is irrelevant to the question.

Many interpreters, however, have falsely said or implied that the *Cratylus* does oppose nature to law. Steinthal did this, and prefaced his discussion of the *Cratylus* with a considerable discussion of the law-nature opposition in Greek literature. He ludicrously misrepresents the dialogue when he writes '*νόμῳ*, das heisst *ἀπ' αὐτομάτου*'. Apelt wrote that 'one sees that the whole controversy revolves round the question whether speech arose *φύσει* or *νόμῳ*, and that is precisely the question that Plato's dialogue not only starts with but considers throughout' (p. 4). Taylor wrote that 'the issue under consideration is thus only one aspect of the famous "sophistic" antithesis between "nature" and "social usage" which we know to have been the great controversial issue of the Periclean age' (*Plato the Man and his Work*, ed. 2, p. 77).

This common mistake is probably due partly to the prominence of the idea of contrasting law with nature in other Greek literature, including some of Plato's other works, and partly to the unfortunate fact that the first use of the word '*νόμοι*' in the *Cratylus* happens to be an atypical use of it, unique in the dialogue, in a speech by someone who is scraping up as many ways as possible of saying that there is no natural rightness of names.

'But, though Plato does not here oppose law to nature, yet perhaps the contrast he is making is just the usual contrast between law and nature, only expressed in other terms.' Let us consider this possibility.

The ancient Greeks mostly used the antithesis νόμος-φύσις to distinguish between what men think to be so and what really is so, and to suggest that what men think to be so (in some particular case) is not so. We often use the words 'real', 'really', 'in reality', 'actually', 'true', 'in truth', for the same purpose.

This is a purely formal distinction, and can be applied in any sphere whatever. Anything whatever can be represented as being the real state of affairs, in contrast to somebody's mistaken opinion, if we wish to do so. We can introduce the word 'actually' into every statement we make without altering its sense, and many English schoolgirls did so in the nineteen-forties. Thus Plato could, if he had wished, have made any or each of his characters represent his own view as giving what is actually the case, φύσει, while his opponents give only what is commonly thought to be the case, νόμῳ. But he did not. No speaker in the *Cratylus* ever uses either the word 'φύσει' or the word 'νόμῳ' as a way of representing his own view as the true one in contrast to the mistaken opinions of others.

Some of the ancient Greeks had a favourite sphere in which to apply this formal contrast between what is real and what people think real. This was the sphere suggested by another meaning of the word 'νόμος', namely legal and moral rules. They used this distinction to discredit the reigning legal and moral rules by suggesting that they go contrary to what is really right, and that they imply falsehoods. What the laws say is just is not just in reality; it is right for a man to take what he can get, and wrong for him to be hindered from doing so by legal or moral rules (Plato's 'Callicles', *Go.* 482–9, esp. 484A). This is the most prominent use of the distinction φύσις-νόμος in Greek literature, and the usual one if there is a usual one. It is prominent in Plato's *Gorgias*, and appears also in his *Republic* (358–9) and *Protagoras* (337) and *Laws* (889E–892C).

In Plato's *Cratylus*, on the contrary, no person ever throws doubt on the reigning legal and moral rules, either by using the words 'φύσει-νόμῳ' or in any other way.

There was another use of the antithesis φύσις-νόμος in ancient Greece, less common than the former, namely, to distinguish between things that exist independently of man's thoughts and perceptions and things that exist only in dependence on man's thoughts and perceptions. We often use the words 'objective-subjective' for the same purpose. 'Subjective is hot, subjective is cold, subjective is colour, in reality are atoms and void: νόμῳ θερμόν, νόμῳ ψυχρόν, νόμῳ χροιή, ἐτεῇ δὲ ἄτομα καὶ κενόν', Democritus, B 9, Diels. 'About the noble and the just there is much disagreement and bewilderment, so that they seem to be merely subjective, not objective: νόμῳ μόνον εἶναι, φύσει δὲ μή' Aristotle, *Nic. Eth.* 1094b16.

The question in the *Cratylus* is a question of this sort. It is the question whether the correctness of names is something that exists by nature, independently of what man may think or do, or on the contrary exists only because of what man thinks or does, and hence in dependence thereon. The question in the *Cratylus* could, therefore, be expressed with the aid of the word 'νόμῳ' in contrast with 'φύσει', and it once is (384D). All the rest of the time, however, the dialogue has another and an incompatible use for the word 'νόμος', and hence does not use the opposition φύσει-νόμῳ to express its question.

In sum, the *Cratylus* does not use the words 'φύσει-νόμῳ' to make the distinction they were most commonly used to make, namely that between reality and what people mistakenly think reality to be; nor does it use either these words or this distinction in the way they were most commonly used, namely to throw doubt on reigning legal and moral rules; but it does make the distinction between existing independently of man and existing in dependence on him (e.g. 386DE), and once by exception it expresses this distinction by means of the word '*νόμῳ*'.

I pass to a third proposition which the speakers do not hold to be entailed by the nature-theory, although some may be inclined to think that it is. We might suppose the nature theory to entail that there is *only one correct name* for each thing, and so that all actual languages, excepting at most one, are incorrect. But according to the speakers in the *Cratylus* this does not follow. The syllables may vary without the correctness of the name being necessarily impaired (389D–390A). The Greek and the barbarian lawgiver may both have established the correct name, although their products sound different. Every single letter in a name can be changed without its necessarily becoming incorrect (394B). The right name being the name that shows the essence of the thing, there is more than one way of doing that (393D1–4). For instance, 'Astyanax' and 'Hector' are the same name (394BC); they mean the same and have the same force.

This doctrine of what I may call the indifference of the syllables is disconcerting to me, and I imagine to most of my contemporaries. (It is, of course, an entirely different sense of 'same name' from that in which a contemporary philologist might say that 'mother' and 'Mutter' are the same name. 'Socrates' is not talking here about the evolution of one name-form from another, or about the evolution of one name into two differently sounding names used in different places.) It seems to make the name into a ghost that may take any form, which seems to entail that 'Socrates' can have no way of apprehending this ghost, or of distinguishing between correct and incorrect embodiments of it. I have difficulty in believing that Plato thought it worth while to draw attention to such an absurdity. Nevertheless, I think the doctrine *is* put forward (in 389D–390A and 393–4), and 'Socrates' is made to be confident that he can know when the ghostly name is correctly expressed and when not. For example, in

393E he says you can *see* that the presence of the letters '-eta' does not prevent the name 'beta' from showing the nature of the letter B. I should object that the name 'beta' is a special case, in that the name itself contains the nominate, and so can throw no light on the vast majority of names that do not contain their own nominates; but there is no trace of this thought in the text.

Fourthly, the nature-theory of names does not entail that we can and should learn about things from their names. 'Cratylus' is inclined to think it does entail this, and that is part of why he is enthusiastic about the theory. But 'Socrates' shows him that that is not so, in the last or last but one part of the dialogue, which is also the most serious part. 'Socrates' points out that his earlier attempts to demonstrate a natural correctness in some particular names can be offset by other names that contravene the principles suggested (434DE, 437); that in fact what makes us understand each other is custom, which works whether the customary name resembles its nominate or fails to do so (435B); that names for the numbers apparently must be non-resembling and merely customary (435B); that for all we know our actual names may have been established by someone who was mistaken about the nature of things (436B–D); that, if the first namemaker did know the true natures of things, he must have learned them by some means other than their names (438E); and that it is better to learn about things from themselves than from images of them, which is what names are on the nature-theory (439AB).

Such are the contents and implications of the nature-theory of names propounded in the *Cratylus.*

6

A CRITICISM OF PLATO'S
CRATYLUS

(*First printed in* The Philosophical Review *in 1956*)

In an article in the *Revue Internationale de Philosophie*, 1955, I have described the nature-theory of names which Plato made his 'Socrates' develop in the *Cratylus*, to wit, that 'everything has a right name by nature' (383A). In the present article I first ask whether Plato himself believed the nature-theory of names and then criticize the theory.

Did Plato himself believe the nature-theory of names which he makes his 'Socrates' develop in the *Cratylus*? Perhaps we should ask first whether it is reasonable for us to venture any answer at all on this matter. Perhaps we ought to renounce trying to say whether Plato believed the nature-theory of names. Plato was a dramatist and thought of himself as such; and the business of a dramatist with ideas is to present them, not to judge them. And the dramatic play of ideas is more prominent in the *Cratylus* even than in the *Phaedo*. Only in the *Cratylus* does Plato's protagonist argue against each in turn of two contrarily disposed respondents. The *Cratylus* more than any other of Plato's dialogues except the *Parmenides* justifies Professor Robert's remark that Plato like Rabelais was a mystifier, '*le plus génial mystificateur de tous les temps*' (*Congrès Budé* on Plato and Rabelais [1953], p. 418). The *Cratylus* gives the impression of putting forward ideas for consideration without deciding which of them are true. To deposit ideas in the public domain and to examine them is what it represents 'Socrates' as proposing to do (384C7) and itself in effect does. It is easy to regard the dialogue as showing Plato in a difficulty, unable to say a confident yes or no to a certain proposition. Furthermore, the end of the dialogue is like a way of saying that we have not got to the bottom of the matter and that it needs further study. 'Cratylus' and 'Socrates' tell each other to keep on inquiring and to let each other know if they discover anything.

These considerations might well lead a reasonable man to suspend judgement permanently on the question whether Plato himself believed the nature-theory of names. On the other side, there is some evidence suggesting an answer to the question, as follows:

The theory, that the right name for a thing is a natural revelation of the essence of that thing, is deeply attractive to many people. It explains the fact that we often feel as if the name had the same qualities as its nominate. The word 'ugly' sounds ugly. The word 'beautiful' sounds beautiful. The true name of a terrible god would be so terrible that it is far better not to inquire what it is. (See S. N. Behrman in *The Worcester Account*.) Pigs are rightly called 'pigs'. Civil servants demand their victims' 'true names' and 'full names', refusing to admit that a person's name is what he calls himself.

Plato shared this feeling that a thing has a true name and that the name has the same qualities as the thing. If one thing is more honourable than another, its name is also more honourable than the name of that other (*Phaedrus*, 244D). Some names are terrible and fearful (*Rp.* 387B). His 'Socrates' confesses to a more than human fear with regard to names of the gods (*Philebus*, 12C). We have here, therefore, a small likelihood that Plato held the nature-theory of names.

On the other hand, it is possible to have this feeling about names and yet to disapprove of the feeling when one comes to make a serious investigation, just as one can be afraid of ghosts in the night in spite of being intellectually convinced that there are no ghosts. And the above evidence about

Plato's *feelings* seems to be outweighed by the following evidence about his *views*.

In several dialogues Plato makes his protagonist express the view that it is possible to go astray in investigation by attaching oneself to the name instead of to the thing, and demand that the company shall attend to the thing rather than to its name. To contradict the name rather than the matter is not dialectic but quarrelling (*Rp.* 454A). 'Our aim is not to say the name; it is to consider the thing named' (*Th.* 177DE). 'An easy-going attitude towards names and expressions, and a not examining them minutely, is not ignoble on most occasions; in fact, the opposite attitude is illiberal, though it is sometimes necessary' (ibid., 184C). 'At present you and I have only the name in common with regard to this creature, and the thing to which we apply the name is perhaps private to each of us; but we ought always to agree on the thing itself by means of logoi rather than merely on the name without a logos' (*Soph.* 218C). 'Good, Socrates; and if you persevere in not taking names seriously, you will appear richer in wisdom as you approach old age' (*Politicus*, 261E).

This detached attitude toward names has probably often been taken by people who also assumed that names have a natural connection with their nominates. It is, however, unreasonable to combine this attitude with this assumption; and those who reflect much on the nature-theory are likely to see the unreasonableness. Plato did reflect much on the nature-theory, for he wrote the *Cratylus*. His contempt for names is therefore some small evidence that he did not hold the nature-theory.

The view that there are by nature correct names for things is never asserted in any work of Plato's besides the *Cratylus*. But the contradictory view, that there is no natural connection between a name and its nominate, is clearly implied, and made the basis of an important argument, in *Letter* VII. 'None of them has a firm name. What is now called curved could just as well be called straight, and what is now called straight could just as well be called curved, and these inter-changed and contrary usages could be just as firm. And the same statement holds of statement, since it is composed of names and expressions: it is never sufficiently firmly firm' (*Letter* VII, 343B). This is a large part of the premiss from which Plato there concludes that if Dionysius had been a true Platonist he would not have written a work of Platonic philosophy. This passage does not use either the word 'nature' or the word 'agreement'; but it is hardly compatible with the nature-theory of names in the *Cratylus*, and a person who had written the *Cratylus* would probably notice that. *Letter* VII is also out of sympathy with the nature-theory when it complains of 'the weakness of language' (343A1) and of 'the bad nature' of names and statements (343D8).

Plato's greatest pupil laid it down from the beginning that 'a name is a sound that is significant by convention. . . . I say by convention, because no name exists by nature. Nothing is a name until it becomes a symbol. Merely showing something does not constitute a name. Wordless noises show something, for example the noises of beasts; but none of them is a name' (*De Interp.* 16a19–29).

The above evidence suggests that Plato believed that there is no natural rightness of names. The *Cratylus* itself suggests the same after we have critically examined and weighed the arguments which his 'Socrates' there produces. For the considerations which 'Socrates' finally brings forward against the nature-theory (434–9) are upon reflection un-deniable truths. The passage is as adamantine an argument as you can find anywhere in Plato. It certainly is custom that enables us to understand each other when we do; and the power of custom certainly is wholly independent of whether the name we use resembles its nominate or not; and, however much names might resemble things, it certainly must be possible to learn about things otherwise than from their names; and it must be better to do so. I feel sure that every reasonable man who reflects on these matters to the extent of writing or studying the *Cratylus* becomes convinced of these propositions, and therefore that Plato became convinced of them.

But these propositions have an obvious bearing on the importance and interest of the nature-theory of names. They entail that this theory is rather unimportant and rather uninteresting at best. Whatever remnants of truth 'Socrates'' remarks may have left to it, he has at any rate completely destroyed its pretensions to provide a respectable method of getting to know the world, or even a respectable account of actual names. In fact, there seems to be nothing left of it but a vain regret: 'Perhaps as far as possible it would be best if all or most of our names were like their nominates.' (435C. Méridier seems mistaken in rendering '*ἴσως*' by '*sans doute*'.) The agreement-theory is 'vulgar' (435C); but, 'Socrates' seems to imply, it is inevitable. Throughout the conversation he had refrained from adopting the nature-theory himself, rejecting 'Hermogenes'' imputation of it to him (391A cancels our natural inference from 390E1) and representing all his inventions as inspirations from Euthyphro.

I conclude with some confidence that, while Plato may have entertained the nature-theory favourably before he wrote the *Cratylus*, and even while writing it, he soon came to see that it had no practical use, and he finally came to the convention-theory implied in his *Letter* VII and stated by Aristotle. His writing of the *Cratylus* may have been a sort of purgation of the nature-theory from his mind, whether or not he already expected it to be so when he made his 'Socrates' talk of purging the inspiration of Euthyphro (396E).

Someone may object, however, that, if Plato on completing the *Cratylus* had rejected the nature-theory of names, he would have answered the arguments in favour of that theory which he makes his 'Socrates' develop in the early part of the dialogue. Let us consider this objection.

It cannot be a fatal objection, because Plato makes his 'Socrates' answer neither the arguments which he brings for the theory at the beginning of the dialogue nor the arguments which he brings against it at the end. The suggestion that Plato must have believed the nature-theory because he did not refute the arguments he developed for it is, therefore, neutralized by the suggestion that he must have disbelieved it because he did not refute the arguments he developed against it.

It is worth while, however, to examine the arguments for the nature-theory to see whether they are as strong as the arguments against it, and whether they would have appeared so to Plato. The first argument is that, since statements have a truthvalue, their parts, including names, must have a truthvalue too. Therefore names are true or false (385BC). The argument appears to end here, without explicitly arriving at the nature-theory. But we seem to be expected to think that the view that there is a natural correctness of names follows from the view that names are true or false. In other words, the natural rightness of a name is its being true, and its natural wrongness is its being false.

This argument is bad; for names have no truthvalue, and the reason given for saying that they do is a fallacy of division. No one in the dialogue points out that it is bad; and 'Socrates' makes the converse mistake of composition later on (431B). Nevertheless it is fairly probable that Plato saw or at least felt that it is a bad argument, quite different in quality from those he later produces against the nature-theory. In his *Sophist* (263AB) he said that truthvalue is a character of statements and that statements divide into names and predicates (ὀνόματα καὶ ῥήματα, 262C), and he did not say that names have a truthvalue.

The second argument is: Men differ in goodness and

badness; therefore men differ in wisdom and folly; therefore things have a firm nature of their own independently of us; therefore actions have a firm nature of their own and can be done well only in the way that is natural to them; therefore speech can be done well only in the way that it is natural for things to be said; therefore naming must be done in the way it is natural for things to be named (386–7).

This is a vague argument rather than a bad one. There is something in it; but it is by no means clear precisely what, or whether what there is in it is precisely what is needed to establish the nature-theory. For example, is naming here using an existing name, or inventing a new name, or both? And again, what kind of nature is in question here? The 'natural' way of speaking sounds suspiciously like the customary way of speaking, in which case this is not an argument for the nature-theory of names at all. This argument, therefore, though not without suggestiveness, has nothing like the undeniable quality of the final arguments against the nature-theory. Its element of truth seems more like an assertion of the custom-theory maintained by 'Socrates' at the end of the dialogue.

The third argument is this: the name is the instrument by which we inform each other and distinguish how things are; like all instruments it is given to us by its maker, in this case the lawgiver, and its making requires technical knowledge (388). The competent lawgiver makes a name by looking to 'that itself which is name' and embodying this form in sounds and syllables; for that is the way in which all good tools must be made (389). And his work is directed by the appropriate overseer, namely the dialectician (390).

This argument is not so much an argument as a free development of the nature-theory on the assumption that a name is a tool like a shuttle. It contains no undeniable observations like those which attack the nature-theory at the end of the dialogue. It all rests on the easily deniable assumption that a name is a tool like a shuttle. There are tools which we have to make before we can use them, including the shuttle. There are organs which we do not make but possess as parts of our physical equipment, including the hand. A name is rather more like a hand than a shuttle. But it is very different from both; for it belongs to that third realm, neither nature nor artifact but culture. It is acquired, like a shuttle, but unconstructed, like a hand. Plato, although he has been called a fine sociologist, probably saw little of this; but he probably did see that the argument is weak and fanciful and little more than a fairy tale, in contrast with the hard facts that he produces against the nature-theory at the end. He probably did see that the whole notion of the lawgiver and of the name as like a tool is unsuitable in view of that supremacy of custom in speech which he points out at the end. He probably felt that custom, which he failed to distinguish from agreement, by its role in language excluded the possibility of a name's being a tool like a shuttle, just as Aristotle implies that for a name to exist by agreement is for it not to be a tool (*De Interp.* 17a1).

I conclude that the appearance of Plato's distributing himself equally on both sides of the question is deceptive. In favour of the nature-theory he produces only arguments that are weak or bad; against it he produces unchallengeable arguments; and he probably felt this himself. This was the view of Wilamowitz.[1] George Grote, however, who was a perceptive and judicious interpreter of Plato, thought that Plato at the end of his *Cratylus* was still believing that names having natural rectitude were possible and desirable, though not actual.[2]

I pass now to some other comments on the nature-theory of names and on the manner in which it is discussed by the characters in the *Cratylus*.

[1] U. von Wilamowitz-Moellendorff, *Platon* (Berlin, 1948), Aufl. 4, S. 223.
[2] G. Grote, *Plato* (London, 1865), II, 543.

The nature-theory of names expresses and confirms our desire to see ourselves as reasonable beings. To say that names are right is to say that they are reasonable and there is a reason why a thing has the name it has. There lies behind the nature-theory a tendency to believe that man has a reason for everything he does, or at least ought to have a reason for it. A sound ought not to be connected to a thing merely by being used by men to designate the thing. Men ought to use, in order to designate the thing, some sound that has some natural connection with the thing apart from their use of it. If there were no reason why a thing had the name it had, names would be arbitrary, irrational, pointless, and inexplicable. And if that were so, man, the user of names, would himself be arbitrary and irrational in his language. He would have no reason for the way he talked. Playwrights, when they cannot untie their plots, are tempted to bring in a god on a machine. And we, when we cannot explain a name, are tempted to put it down to the gods or to a foreign language or to 'antiquity'. But those are all nothing but fine excuses. We ought to give a reason (λόγον διδόναι, 425D–426A) for the name.

Thus the nature-theory of names was part of what we may vaguely call Greek rationalism, that is, of a hopeful view of the powers of human reason and the extent to which it really controls human action. It was part of a unique climate of opinion in which human reason seemed to be limited neither as previously, by mysterious gods and customs, nor as now, by mysterious customs and unconscious desires.

We can never again believe in reason as confidently as the Greek philosophers did. But we still try to hide from ourselves the accidental element in language, just as pathetically as Plato's characters do in his *Cratylus*. We still try to show 'reasons' why a given thing should be named by a given name. We hate to make a sheerly new sound, even when we have a sheerly new thing to name, for to do so would expose the arbitrary and irrational element in language. Hence in making a new name we nearly always profess to be using an old description. Even in christening a child, we prefer to use an already existing name, and we laugh at or repudiate those innovators who invent entirely new names.

The speakers in the *Cratylus* tend to assume that names are either entirely reasonable or entirely arbitrary, and that they will be driven to the latter position if they yield the former. But the fact is that, although there is no natural correctness of names independent of man, there nevertheless is a correctness of names and of other aspects of speech. Some utterances are definitely correct, and some are definitely incorrect. The nature-theory looks for this correctness in a wrong place; but it does not look for a non-existent correctness. On the one hand, the name of a thing does not belong to it by nature; on the other hand, a name can be correct or incorrect. On the one hand, we scholars see that there is no natural connection between a thing and its name; on the other hand, people constantly ask us which name is correct, and they are right to do so.

I proceed to try to give a better account of the real correctness of a name. Many rules and standards and principles may bear on a single act, and so it may be correct or incorrect in many different ways; and this applies to any particular utterance of a name. But if we seek to realize those aspects of its correctness or incorrectness which belong to it in virtue of its being a name, we must find its purpose as a name. The goodness or badness of a name and the rightness or wrongness of a use of it depend on the purpose of names in general, of this particular name, and of this particular utterance of this particular name. The correctness of a name depends on the answer to the question: what do we want from this name, and what character will make it best do what we want it to do? 'It is by criteria derived from consideration of the requirements of the referring task that we should assess the adequacy of any system of naming.'[1]

The speakers in the *Cratylus* fail to hold firmly in mind that the correctness of a name depends on its purpose. At first it seems that they fully grasp this point, for they call the name a tool and compare it with the shuttle, the knife, and other tools (387–8); and they explicitly ask what we do with the name and answer that we use it to teach each other and to distinguish how things are (388B). Yet the notion of a purpose or τέλος was invented by Aristotle, not by Plato. And Plato in the *Cratylus* does not use his notion of mark or σκοπός, nor his notion of function or ἔργον. (The word 'ἔργον' in the *Cratylus* means a product, never a function.) And as his 'Socrates' develops the notion that the name is a tool, it turns into something oddly remote from our conception of the purpose of a tool. Instead of the purpose of the tool, he talks of the Form or εἶδος of the tool; and this Form is something which we are supposed to apprehend telepathically, without any means of doing so. We are explicitly forbidden to learn from experience what form a shuttle should take: 'If his shuttle breaks as he is making it, will he in making another look to the broken one, or to that Form to which he also looked in making the broken one? To the Form, I think' (389A). The inquiry what we do with a name (388B) turns into the contemplation of That Itself which a Name is (389D). The practical study of the business of talking turns into the mystic vision of an object which there are no directions for finding. It is like trying to find out why a hammer should be heavy in the head without considering the use of a hammer. While correctly using the analogy of cutting to show that there is a right and wrong in names (387A), 'Socrates' fails to remark that the rightness of a knife depends on the purpose you have in mind. While correctly saying that the carpenter tries to make an ideal shuttle, he implies that what constitutes an ideal shuttle is nothing to do

[1] P. F. Strawson, 'On Referring', *Mind*, N.S., lix (1950), 341.

with its purpose or its success in achieving that purpose. On the contrary, he says that he has shown that our intention has nothing to do with it: 'Not such as he may wish, but such as nature demands' (389C). He does not see that until someone wishes for something there is no end, and therefore no means to an end, and therefore no tool either good or bad. Our wish is in the very word 'shuttle'. Nothing is a shuttle unless someone wishes to weave cloth. The 'nature' to which 'Socrates' feels we must submit is in the means, not in the end. Given that we wish for a certain end, then it is no longer a matter of our wishes what is the best means to achieve that end. Thus the correctness and incorrectness of names, far from being independent of us and inconsistent with names' depending on us, depends on our having purposes which we try to fulfil by means of names. A name is correct and a use of a name is correct, roughly speaking, if with it we can achieve the purposes of language, whatever they are, and without it we cannot. It is correct to use the name '*ail*' for garlic in France, if by using this name you can easily buy garlic in France whereas without this name it is difficult.

It is a strange fact that people rarely appeal to the purposes of language when defending the correctness of a piece of language or defending the doctrine that there is some correctness in language. The reason why Humpty Dumpty cannot do what he says he can do, namely make words mean what he likes, is that that would prevent him from communicating with other people, which is the main purpose of language. But it is not only children like Alice who fail to see that this is the reason and are confined to dogmatic disagreement with him. Nor is it only ancients like Plato's 'Socrates' who appeal instead to an undetectable Form of the word. What language must be in order to be any *use* is very rarely part of people's early reflections on language.

What is the purpose of a name? The persons of Plato's *Cratylus* fail to see that this question is the key to the correctness of names, and they fail to put the question explicitly (except for the abortive 388B already discussed). Nevertheless, they imply an answer to it. Their answer is false, and that is the great cause of their failure to discover the real correctness of names.

The purpose of a name is to refer us to a thing. The purpose of making a name is to have a means of referring people to something, and the purpose of using the name is to refer someone to it. If you say 'Westminster Abbey', you refer your hearer to the Abbey, and you can then go on to describe it to him. If he asks, 'What about it?' you can say, 'It is falling down'. The statement 'Westminster Abbey is falling down' describes something; and part of the way in which it does so is that it includes a name which refers to that thing. The description of a thing referred to is done by the statement as a whole; but the reference is done by one part of it, the name, and can be done by the name uttered alone. Both proper and general names refer. Proper names refer definitely to some one particular as such. General names refer indefinitely to one or some or any or all of a set of things.

It is not the job of a name to describe. The job of a name is to refer; and reference is not description, and does not usually describe (though it may describe, as in 'that tall man over there'). The utterance of a thing's name does not tell the hearer what the thing is. It only refers him to the thing. It is true that names often suggest descriptions. The name 'Gerald' suggests that the nominate is a man. But the suggestion is inessential so long as the word remains a name. A person may call his bad knee 'Gerald'. A woman may be christened 'Gerald'. Humpty Dumpty was wrong to say that a name must mean something.

Since a name does not describe its nominate, there cannot be a 'contradiction between the conventional names and the true essences of things'. All that can happen is that the description of the thing accidentally suggested by its name may be false. Names do not state the essences of their nominates either falsely or truly; they merely name their nominates, that is, refer to them.

There is a strong feeling that names *ought* to describe as well as to designate. To christen a new thing with an entirely new sound which does not suggest any description is commonly felt to be improper, probably because it brings the arbitrary side of language into prominence. Yet it is convenient to separate the referring function from the describing function, because the description may turn out to be wrong. For example, after we have named a certain species of umbellifer *'gigans'*, a bigger species may turn up.

Instead of the feeling that names *ought* to describe as well as to designate, we find sometimes the assumption that names do describe and only describe. We find that the proper function of a name is hardly recognized at all, and instead the name is thought of as if it were a little statement and had the same descriptive function as a statement. This view perhaps lies at the back of the doctrine that all language is metaphorical. It is certainly an essential part of the nature-theory of names in the *Cratylus*.

Early in the *Cratylus*, 'Socrates' approximates names to statements by asserting that, if statements are true or false, names are true or false also (385C). In fact, statements are true or false because they describe and assert; and names are neither true nor false because they do not assert or describe, but name or refer.

In the only place where the 'Socrates' of the *Cratylus* explicitly asks what we do with a name, the answer he gives himself is false, because it would be a true account of what we do with a statement, and the function of a statement is not the same as the function of a name. To say that 'a name is a tool whose use is to inform each other and to distinguish how things are' (388B) is wrong in the same way as it would be wrong to say that 'a carburettor is a tool whose use is to get from place to place'. The use of the carriage is to get from place to place, and the carburettor is part of the carriage; but the use of the carburettor is not the use of the carriage. Similarly, the use of the statement is to inform each other and distinguish how things are, and the name is part of the statement; but the use of the name is not the use of the statement.

All of the great quantity of etymologizing in the dialogue consists in trying to show of each name in turn that it gives a true description of its nominate and was chosen as its name for that reason. Compare, for example, 'the essence of the thing revealed in the name' (393D); 'what the name means' (397E); 'what opinion they were holding when they imposed names on things' (401A). The speakers assume that every ὄνομα is an ἐπωνυμία, every name is a description. They speak of the βούλησις or meaning of the name (421B), which is something different from its nominate. They sum up their etymologizing by saying: 'In the names that we have gone through, the correctness was intended to be such as to show what sort of thing each of the realities is' (422D). They ask how the primary names will make things as plain to us as possible, and they seem to imply that names must do this in order to be really names (εἴπερ μέλλει ὀνόματα εἶναι, 422E). 'The rightness of a name is that which will show what the thing is. . . . Names are uttered for the sake of information' (428E). The rightness of a name is 'to be a revelation of a thing in syllables and letters' (433B). 'The name is a revelation of the thing' (433D). 'The force of a name is to teach' (435D).

When we realize that reference is distinct from description and that the business of a name is not to describe but to refer, the point of looking for enlightenment in etymologies vanishes. Any description suggested by the name is irrelevant, even if the name was deliberately invented by some 'onomast' with that description in mind. Whether the man who invented the word 'gas' had chaos in mind as a true description of gas is pleasant historical gossip, but nothing to do with the business of the word.

From the account of the name as a description or revelation or δήλωμα, the speakers are led to conceive it as an imitation or μίμημα (423B, 430A, E), or εἰκών (439A); and so 'Socrates'' good remarks on the nature of an image (423–432) come to be at the same time an elaborately false account of the nature of a name. To imitate is not to name or indicate or mention. A child imitates the behaviour of the people around him, and in so doing he is not mentioning their behaviour. Imitation is occasionally used as a way of referring; but it is an inconvenient way of referring, used only when nothing better is available. Names are not imitations, but a distinct and much better means of referring to things. In referring to a thing by its name we are making use of a custom instead of an imitation. We imitate things with our bodies only when we are deprived of a customary nonimitative means of referring to them. The tourist in Denmark imitates a man drinking beer only when he cannot think of the Danish name for beer.

Though 'Socrates' makes damaging remarks about the nature-theory in the last part of the dialogue, he never clearly points out this most fundamental falsehood of the theory: that it assumes that the business of a name is to describe its nominate, whereas it is merely to refer to that nominate. (I think it is impossible to say this unambiguously in Platonic Greek.) He never says that we cannot learn about things from their names because things are not described by their names. He says only that it is risky and unsatisfactory to try to learn about things from their names because they may be incorrectly described by their names (435–7, esp. 436B). Even while making the point that many names are in fact unlike their nominates and work by custom or convention or agreement, he still thinks of the name as a 'showing' of the thing (δήλωμα ... δήλωμα ... δηλοῖ ... δήλωσιν, 435AB).

Did Plato ever realize the distinction between reference and description and see that the function of names is to refer? Not in any decisive or unmistakable fashion. There is, however, a tendency toward this realization both in the *Theaetetus* and in the *Sophist*. 'Each [of the prime elements] itself by itself would be nameable only, not otherwise describable either as existing or as not existing.' ('Ονομάσαι μόνον εἴη, προσειπεῖν δὲ οὐδὲν ἄλλο δυνατόν. *Th.* 201E.) The distinction is suggested here and also on the next page with its distinction between ὄνομα and λόγος. But the point is not developed or firmly grasped; it only floats up for a moment as part of a discussion of the relative knowability of simples and compounds. (The passage assumes the falsehood that simples are indescribable; but that is irrelevant to the question to what extent it grasps the distinction between description and reference.)

The distinction appears again in the *Sophist*, and more clearly and accurately. 'When someone says "man understands", that you say is a statement, the smallest and first?— I do.—Because, presumably, he is now revealing [δηλοῖ] something about things that are or were or will be. He is not merely naming. He is completing something, by combining expressions with names. Hence we say he is stating, not merely naming; and to this combination we have assigned the name "statement".—Right' (*Soph.* 262D). It does not follow, however, that had Plato then gone back to the discussion of names as such, he would have avoided the *Cratylus'* error of regarding them as little statements. It often happens that we imply the right view of a thing when we mention it incidentally, and yet give a wrong account when we discuss it for its own sake.

There is one further indistinction to mention as contributing to the defectiveness of the *Cratylus'* account of names: it fails to realize the difference between establishing a name and using a name. It is one thing to baptize a baby 'John' and another thing to refer to him as John thereafter. It is one thing to lay down a meaning for the word 'deuterium' and another thing to use the word thereafter. The two things both admit of correctness and incorrectness, since they are both human actions; but their criteria of correctness are different. The failure of Plato's persons to find the real correctness of names is partly due to their failure to hold this difference in mind. The largest part of the dialogue, with its mass of etymologies, is an attempt to justify the supposed original *establishment* of the names discussed; but in 429–31 'Socrates' argues that there can be such a thing as an incorrect *use* of an established name, and the speakers are not aware that they have changed the subject.

We cannot see the real correctness of names unless we consider separately the correctness of their establishment and of their use. The correct use of names, to take that first, consists almost entirely in using the customary name in the customary way. That is because the function of names is to refer, and if we do not use the customary name in the customary way, we commonly fail to refer our hearers to that to which we want to refer them. Where two customary names are available, the choice between them on any particular occasion may be indifferent, or one of them may be incorrect and the other correct, as for example when one is obscene and the other not. (Obscenity may also effect that the correct thing is not to use a name at all, but to refer by a roundabout phrase or a euphemism.) Since customs vary from group to group, the correct name varies from group to group, from place to place, from time to time. Sometimes it is obvious what the correct name to use is; occasionally it is very dubious and there is no satisfactory answer. The wise man respects all customs and follows the custom of those to whom he is speaking. (Among the exceptions to this rule is the case where his hearers, for some special reason, expect him as a matter of propriety to follow a different custom which they understand but do not themselves use.)

The yoke of custom is very heavy in the matter of using names. Most departures from it are summarily punished by unintelligibility, failure to communicate. Those who, discontented with the arbitrariness, or what they sometimes call the 'illogicality' of an actual name, try to use something more 'rational', become ridiculous or worse. The truly correct, the truly 'logical' name is after all the customary name.

This custom, or νόμος, which strictly limits our successful speaking, is not the work of any lawgiver, or νομοθέτης. We cannot thank or reproach any original namemaker for it. It is part of the great web of culture in which we are held, which we did not make or choose, which we can do little to alter, which we must teach to our children, much of which we can and should learn to love, but much of which, alas, is quite unlovable. So much on correctness in the use of names.

Sometimes new names are successfully made. That is, a new custom is, by deliberate human contrivance, added to the multitude of reigning customs constituting a living language. The word 'kodak', which is now a customary part of the English language, was deliberately introduced by G. Eastman (according to the *S.O.E.D.*); and I have been told that he aimed at inventing a sound which could be used in different languages. The joke, that an American college president announced that 'from today it will be a tradition that . . .', is popular in England because the English underestimate, and the Americans overestimate, the extent to which human enterprise can deliberately alter human custom and culture.

As to correctness in the invention of names, it is a far more fluid affair than correctness in the use of them; and a far wider area is left open to arbitrary choice. Once we have escaped from the idea that correctness in the invention of

names could be the correct description of their nominates, we
see that there is no overwhelming, all-disposing principle of
correctness in this field, and that to a large extent we are left
without any guidance and are compelled to make arbitrary
choices. The criteria that determine a good name leave far
more things indifferent than the criteria that determine a
good knife; and the arbitrary element in language appears
nearly naked here.

That there must be much arbitrariness in the invention of
new names is concealed through most of the *Cratylus* by the
assumption that the business of a name is to describe its
nominate. But the doctrine appears, in a distorted version, in
'Socrates'' peculiar view that the form of a name can be the
same in different syllables: 'If not every lawgiver embodies
the name in the same syllables, we must not forget this: not
every smith embodies the tool in the same iron, though he
makes it for the same purpose' (389DE, retaining the difficult ἀγνοεῖν; cf. 393–4). There is no single form which the
sound must have in order to be a name of the thing.[1]

Yet there are rules or principles for good name-making as
well as for good name-using. The fact that the job of a name
is not to describe by no means involves that it can be made
anyhow, or that any name is as good as any other name. A
name has a definite use, and anything that has a definite use
can be made better or worse for its use. Names need to be
short and easily pronounceable, yet distinct from other
words. They need to fit well into the phonic and grammatical
systems of the language and into the spirit of the language
which its customary users vaguely feel. Several principles of
name-making are suggested in my *Definition*, pages 80–92,
under the head of 'rules for stipulative definition'; for

[1] 1969. I now think that the MS. reading is meaningless. I adopt
Burnet's text with Peipers' ἀμφιγνοεῖν and translate: 'If not every
lawgiver puts it into the same syllables, this should cause no uncertainty;
for neither does every smith put it into the same iron when he makes the
same tool for the same purpose.'

stipulative definition is the establishment or attempted establishment of a new name. I will not repeat them here, but merely add, in conclusion, the two following remarks.

1. We should probably acknowledge the arbitrary element in language more than we do; for that would encourage us to invent new sounds for our new names, instead of taking an old sound and thus creating a new ambiguity.

2. I have suggested in my *Definition*[1] that 'perhaps we ought not to stipulate unless we are in some sense authorities in the field to discuss which we stipulate'. This may recall the statement in the *Cratylus* that 'not everyone is a maker of names' (390E). But against the *Cratylus* I wish to say that the proper maker of names is neither the dialectician (unless it is a name for use in dialectic) 'nor he who looks to the name in nature of each thing' (390E). The proper maker of names is in each field the influential and well-placed authority in that field; for only he has both the knowledge of what things need to be named and the authority to impose his names.

[1] Oxford, 1950, p. 92.

7

ARISTOTLE ON ACRASIA

(*'L'acrasie selon Aristote'*, composed in French, was delivered as a lecture at the Sorbonne on 7 April 1954, and published in Revue Philosophique in 1955. This translation into English is here first printed.)

ARISTOTLE asks himself in the Seventh Book of his *Nicomachean Ethics* how a man can do what he knows to be wrong. Doing what one knows to be wrong is what he calls 'acrasia'. On the one hand, it seems evident that acrasia occurs from time to time. On the other hand, Socrates declared that knowledge ought to rule in the soul and not be dragged about like a slave. He concluded from this authority of knowledge that in reality acrasia never occurs. Whenever we seem to see a man doing what he knows to be wrong, the truth is that the man does not know that his act is wrong; he is in error about the right and the wrong. This constitutes a difficulty or 'aporia'. The commonsense view that we sometimes do what we know to be wrong appears to contradict the Socratic view, itself also very convincing, that knowledge is commanding.

How does Aristotle resolve this problem? Evidently he did not write nearly a whole book on acrasia in order to deny that it ever occurs. On the contrary, he always retained the common view that we sometimes do what we know to be wrong. This is probably what he is saying, though not without a certain ambiguity, in the passage where he first introduces the Socratic thesis, when he writes (1145b28) that this doctrine obviously goes against appearances and that the acratic clearly does not think so until he is in the passion—meaning, I suppose, that the acratic does not think that his act is permissible until he is in the passion.

But what is the meaning of the mysterious words that come between the two phrases which I have just translated: δέον ζητεῖν περὶ τὸ πάθος, εἰ δὲ ἄγνοιαν, τίς ὁ ρεόπος γίνεται τῆς ἀγνοίας? Are they to be interpreted by reference to the Socratic thesis or by reference to the explanation of acrasia which Aristotle is going to develop in what follows? If we refer them to the Socratic thesis, we suppose that Aristotle is meaning to say to Socrates: 'Since you hold that what we call acrasia is really ignorance, you ought to have told us what kind of ignorance we have here.' If we refer them to the view which Aristotle is about to set out we suppose that Aristotle is here saying, though so succinctly as to be almost incomprehensible, that he is going to satisfy Socrates by saying that there is a certain ignorance in acrasia, but at the same time he is going to distinguish the nature of this ignorance so as to preserve the doctrine that the acratic knows that his act is wrong.

Aristotle rejects as unacceptable that solution of the difficulty which consists in saying that the acratic does not *know* that his act is wrong but only *believes* that it is (1145b31 ff.). Aristotle takes this to mean that belief involves a less strong and sure conviction than does knowledge and that it is the weakness of the acratic's conviction which makes it possible for him to disobey it. Aristotle rejects this solution on the ground that the man whose conviction is weak is pardoned, whereas the acratic is blameworthy. He seems to think that this solution amounts to another way of denying that acrasia in the proper sense can occur.

In the following chapter, number 3, Aristotle returns to this supposed solution and rejects it again, but now for a different reason. He now declares (1146b24 ff.) that the distinction between knowledge and belief does not necessarily involve any difference of certainty or conviction. Some who only believe are as certain as some others who know. With the humour that occasionally lightens the sombre theme of this book, Aristotle instances Heraclitus as a man who was perfectly certain although he did not know.

These two ways of rejecting the solution are consistent with each other. One of them attacks the premiss. The other attacks the inference, implying that it is an *ignoratio elenchi*.

Finally Aristotle gives us the four solutions which he considers correct. The first depends on distinguishing the time when we possess a certain piece of knowledge but are not using it from the time when we both possess and are using it. The latter is also called θεωροῦντα, contemplating. Aristotle gives no example of what he has in mind; but no doubt he would have accepted the following. As I begin this sentence, you possess but are not using the knowledge that Greece is an arid land; as I end it, you are using it as well as possessing it, because I have recalled it to your minds. This is part of his great doctrine of potentiality and act, although he uses the word ἐνεργεῖ only twice in this chapter. To say that a man knows something is not to say that he is always thinking of it, nor that he is thinking of it now. Aristotle appears to mean that the acratic knows that his act is wrong in that he *possesses* this knowledge, but he can do the act because he is not at the time *using* this knowledge, not contemplating it. I hold that Aristotle accepts this solution and believes it to contain virtually everything necessary for the explanation of acrasia, since it shows how the acratic both knows and does not know that his act is wrong. He knows it, in that it is part of his permanent and general intellectual equipment. He does not know it, in that he does not use or contemplate it at the moment when he needs to do so, the moment of his acratic act. However, Aristotle adds three more solutions.

The second of these four solutions consists in introducing his doctrine of the practical syllogism. According to Aristotle the motion of the human animal is sometimes governed by a syllogism. When such a motion constitutes a πρᾶξις, that is an action in the proper sense, it is perhaps always governed by a syllogism. Aristotle is never very precise in explaining this syllogism. For example, its conclusion sometimes seems to be an action, but at other times a statement. It is certain enough, however, that the premiss has two parts, one of which is καθόλου or universal and the other καθ'ἕκαστον or particular. The universal premiss gives us a practical principle, such as 'Every sweet thing should be tasted'. It is expressed sometimes by means of the verb δεῖ or the verbal adjective in τέον, but sometimes also by a simple descriptive phrase such as 'Dry things are good for every man', or even 'Everything sweet is pleasant'.

Aristotle's second solution consists in pointing out that it is possible for an agent, while *possessing* both premisses, to *use* only the universal premiss. Such an agent may do an act forbidden by the syllogism. Yet he possesses the forbidding principle, and therefore it is correct to say that he knows that the act is wrong.

Aristotle adds that one can distinguish even more finely. Since the universal premiss will often contain two terms, such as, for example, 'man' and 'dry' in the premiss that 'Dry things are good for every man', it will need as it were two particular premisses to particularize each of these universal terms. Hence it can happen that an agent particularizes one of these terms but not the other. This agent will use both the universal premiss and a part of the particular premiss, and still not do the act which the syllogism prescribes.

We see that the second solution as well as the first consists in showing that the acratic both knows and does not know that his act is wrong. He knows it in that he possesses the principle in virtue of which his act is wrong. He does not know it in that he does not use this principle, or he does use it but he does not use the particular premiss that would put the principle into action, or he even uses part of the particular premiss but not the whole of it.

Let us pass to the third solution. It is again a distinction, a subdivision. Aristotle now subdivides his 'possessing but not using'. A sleeping man and a waking man may both possess the practical principle. But, says Aristotle, the sleeping man possesses it 'in a manner other than those just mentioned' (1147a10); he 'both possesses and does not possess it in a way'. Aristotle adds that such is the condition not merely of the sleeping but also of the mad and the drunk and the acratic. He assimilates acrasia to medical cases. (His ethics has a tendency to turn into medicine.) The acratic can even utter the words which express the knowledge and yet not be using it. For a moment Aristotle almost seems to want to say that during his act the acratic simply does not know; for he uses the expression ἴσασι δ' οὔπω. At any rate, this third solution amounts to saying that during his act the acratic possesses the knowledge that it is wrong only in a most attenuated way.

Thus we find Aristotle tending for the third time to deny that the acratic fully knows the nature of his act while he is committing it. He seems to tend to believe with Socrates that knowledge cannot be outraged, and that it can be disobeyed only when it is not fully present. If we think, as some interpreters do, that in the end Aristotle is going to present acrasia as involving throughout perfect knowledge that the act is wrong, then this third solution at any rate is absolutely absurd and irrelevant. There remains, however, the following substantial difference between Socrates and Aristotle, that Socrates, as far as we know, never entertained the idea that the acratic's state of knowledge might change importantly during the course of the transaction, in that he knew the nature of his act perfectly both before and after but not during the commission of it.

Let us turn to the fourth and last solution. Here is no further distinction of senses of the word 'know'. Aristotle begins by expanding somewhat the nature of the practical syllogism. He brings out now the aspect of necessity in this syllogism. Once the premisses have become one, he says, it is

necessary, ἀνάγκη, to act, to realize the conclusion at once.
What a paradoxical thesis! And what a very Socratic thesis!
I think it the most Socratic sentence in this fundamentally
Socratic chapter. Even if we add, as Aristotle does not, that the
agent knows the two premisses and is thoroughly convinced
of them, the sentence remains extraordinary. In proceeding
to illustrate it he greatly weakens it, for he says now that the
act is necessary 'if one has the ability and is not prevented'
(1147a30); but it remains pretty Socratic and pretty extreme.

What was his purpose in introducing it? Surely not in order
to go on to say that one can do an act while possessing and
fully using a syllogism that forbids that act. It is now very
improbable that the fourth solution is finally going to reject
the Socratic doctrine. I believe on the contrary that he
introduces this practical necessity in order to prove that the
acratic must do the wrong act because of a syllogism which
imposes this wrong act upon him. For he speaks now of the
complicated case where four things are present at once in the
soul. (1) First, there is in the soul a universal premiss which
forbids the man to 'taste', where to 'taste' is probably to
commit the acratic act, while the phrase 'there is in the soul',
ἐνῇ (1147a32), probably means that he possesses this premiss
but is not using it. (2) Second, there is also in the soul another
universal premiss to the effect that everything sweet is
pleasant; and this premiss is actual, ἐνεργεῖ. (3) Third, there is
also the particular premiss that this thing is sweet, a premiss
which can set the second universal premiss into action.
(4) Fourth, there happens to be a desire, ἐπιθυμία, in the soul.

What according to Aristotle is the result of this combination of four things in the soul? He seems to indicate three
consequences. First, the first universal premiss orders the
man to shun this thing; second, desire carries him away; and,
third, it thus results that the acratic act accords in a way with
a logos and an opinion, this opinion being opposed to the
correct logos only accidentally, and not in itself.

This short and vague account makes us ask the following questions. What exactly does the first universal premiss say (for Aristotle does not tell us)? What is the particular premiss belonging to this first universal premiss (for he does not say that either)? And is the first and right syllogism completely actual in the soul of the acratic at the time of his act, or is it not?

I answer as follows. In the other three solutions, and also in the early sentences of this fourth solution, it seemed clear enough that Aristotle was thinking that at the time of his act the acratic is not using in complete actuality every part of the right syllogism. I will suppose, therefore, that here too he thinks that the acratic is not using every part of the right syllogism, provided that the text allows me to do so. Does the text allow me? I see only one phrase that has any appearance of forbidding it, namely the phrase ἢ μὲν οὖν λέγει φεύγειν τοῦτο, 'the [first universal premiss] tells [him] to shun this' (1147a34). But it is not necessary to hold that by these words Aristotle intends to tell us that he is now supposing the right syllogism to be completely actual. The word λέγει is vague enough to mean no more than that the right universal premiss *tends* to forbid the act, and *would* forbid it if joined to its own particular premiss in actuality.

It follows from this interpretation that the particular premiss belonging to the right universal premiss is not the same as the one belonging to the wrong universal premiss. For the latter particular premiss is actual in the acratic's soul. Hence, if the two particular premisses were the same, the right syllogism would be actual in his soul, which on this interpretation it is not.

The particular premiss of the right syllogism is not the same as the particular premiss of the wrong syllogism. What, then, is the particular premiss of the right syllogism? We cannot tell. We can only conjecture. Similarly, therefore, we can only conjecture what is the universal premiss of the right syllogism, which also Aristotle does not tell us.

LEG

The fourth solution continues with a remark about animals, and why they cannot be acratic (1147b4). I confess that I do not see the relevance of this. Possibly there is something hidden in this sentence which would disprove my interpretation if it were revealed.

However that may be, my interpretation is strongly supported by the next phrase, 'how the ignorance is dissipated and the acratic resumes his knowledge' (1147b6). For this phrase undoubtedly implies that some kind of ignorance exists during the acratic act; and one can hardly suppose that it refers merely to the first three solutions. It must imply that this ignorance also occurs in the circumstances supposed in the solution which stands nearest to it in the text, and that is the fourth solution.

The next sentence begins with the words 'Since the last premiss' (1147b9). It seems a little odd to talk of a last premiss when there are only two. Perhaps Aristotle is thinking of a sorites or chain of syllogisms, such as could easily be constructed out of examples which he gave earlier (1147a6–7). In such a chain there would be more than two premisses altogether. In any case this 'last' premiss would be a particular premiss; and Aristotle now tells us that the acratic while 'in the passion' either does not have this premiss or has it only as the drunk has the verses of Empedocles. This is another affirmation of the Socratic thesis that some kind of ignorance occurs during the acratic act; but it is not a strong piece of evidence for the interpretation of the fourth solution, because now, by mentioning the drunken man reciting Empedocles, Aristotle refers us back to the third solution; and he could have forgotten by now the intervening fourth solution.

Aristotle does not say explicitly what the man will do if he has both syllogisms completely actual in his mind, nor whether such a state of mind is possible.

Before beginning his discussion of acrasia, Aristotle had made some remarks on the character that the discussion ought to have (1145b2–7). These five lines are neither the only nor the longest passage in the *Nicomachean Ethics* where Aristotle teaches us what sorts of study ethics and politics are or ought to be. But they illuminate best the method that he tried to follow and the result that he wished to attain. He wishes to establish, if possible, all received opinions, ἔνδοξα. If that is not possible, he wishes to establish as many as he can of the more important received opinions. He limits himself to the removal of difficulties, and leaves standing every opinion that he is not compelled to reject. He will accomplish this design in three stages. First, he will list the opinions. That is to 'posit the appearances' (1145b3); and he performs it in the last part of the first chapter of Book VII. Secondly he will raise the difficulties, τὰς ἀπορίας. He does that in the second chapter. Finally, he will resolve these difficulties, if possible without rejecting any received opinion; in any case he will reject as few of these opinions as he can. He does this in chapters 3 to 10, which constitute the whole of the rest of his discussion of acrasia, and by far the largest part of it.

It is a very modest programme. No grandiose construction. No metaphysic of morals. Aristotle does not look down on common sense. On the contrary, he subjects himself to common sense almost entirely. He thinks of his work as justifying rather than as superseding common sense. He ventures only to raise certain 'unpleasantnesses', δυσχερῆ, and to make a few alterations in order to remove them.

He carries out this programme in regard to acrasia. He notes and accepts the common opinion that acrasia occurs from time to time. That is to say, from time to time men do acts which they know to be wrong, owing to some passion. Then they are 'ecstatic of reason', as he puts it once; and this is a blameworthy state. But he notes also the opinion, maintained in the most striking way by Socrates, that the knowledge a man possesses cannot be overcome, or dragged about like a slave, by anything else in his soul. The words in which he here reports Socrates (1145b24) remind us strongly of the thesis that ἐπιστήμη is something ἡγεμονικόν and ἀρχικόν, which Plato had made his 'Socrates' maintain in his *Protagoras*, 352B. Aristotle accepts this opinion too. What he does not accept is the view that the Socratic thesis is inconsistent with the ordinary opinion that acrasia occurs from time to time. He confines himself to showing, by means of his doctrines of potentiality and of the syllogism, that the two propositions are consistent, so that we are not obliged to reject either of them. He removes the difficulty and leaves the received opinions standing. That is in his view a sufficient demonstration. Δεδειγμένον ἂν εἴη ἱκανῶς (1145b7). For the solution of the difficulty is a discovery, ἡ γὰρ λύσις τῆς ἀπορίας εὕρεσίς ἐστιν, 1146b7. No more extraordinary discovery is to be looked for in this matter.

OBJECTIONS TO THIS INTERPRETATION

Several objections have been made against this interpretation. In the first place, it is objected that, if Aristotle had explained acrasia as I have said he did, he would have left unexplained the most essential and most paradoxical kind of acrasia. For pure essential acrasia occurs, it is said, when a man does wrong although he understands perfectly and completely, at the very moment of doing the act, that it is wrong. That, precisely, is the essence of acrasia, and also the only kind of acrasia that needs explaining. But on my interpretation it appears that the only kind of acrasia that needs explaining is precisely the only kind that Aristotle does not explain. For on my view every one of the four solutions amounts to saying that the acratic, at the time of his act, does not have fully in mind all the parts of the practical syllogism that ought to govern it. And, it is said, one cannot believe that Aristotle was so stupid.

My answer consists of two remarks. I remark first that

everyone agrees that the first three solutions consist in saying that, in one way or another, the acratic does not keep all the parts of the syllogism active in his mind throughout. If then it is true, as the objection declares, that this sort of acrasia does not need to be explained, Aristotle has been in any case pretty stupid in introducing these three solutions. In fact, these interpreters are embarrassed by these three solutions, because in their opinion they do not bear on the real question. They are obliged to use the word 'dialectically', and to declare that Aristotle is here speaking dialectically and when he speaks dialectically he is not serious. But what good reason could Aristotle have had to introduce into his discussion a page that was not serious? I think we do better to suppose that Aristotle is serious in his first three solutions as well as in his last. And from this supposition it follows that Aristotle himself did not consider it superfluous to explain the case where the practical syllogism is partially absent.

In the second place, I deny that Aristotle would have been stupid if he had failed to explain the case in which the practical syllogism is wholly present in the mind of the man who does a wrong act. I believe on the contrary that he would rather have been stupid if he had tried to do that, because this case does not occur. It is a wholly imaginary case, whereas Aristotle wished to explain realities. It does not happen that a man sets himself to consider, in its totality and all its parts, an argument forbidding him to do a certain act, while at the same time he yields to a strong desire and does as the desire wishes. The human mind is not adapted to do two things at the same time while giving full attention to each. During the crisis of his passion the acratic can hardly even remember the words that would express the argument. If by exception he does still remember the words, he does so only like a drunken man reciting verses by Empedocles without understanding them, as Aristotle remarks.

I turn to the second objection to my interpretation. It is in a way an attempt to revive part of the first objection, by saying that, however absurd it may seem to us to set out three solutions that are not serious, Aristotle himself tells us that he has done this, when he introduces his fourth solution with the word φυσικῶς. The fourth solution is indeed described as φυσικῶς. We are told that this implies that the first three failed to reach the nature or φύσις of the thing. And this in turn implies that we must not interpret the fourth solution as introducing once more the feeble idea that the acratic does not have the syllogism wholly present in his mind.

I reply as follows. When we read in the works of Aristotle the eleven cases of φυσικῶς θεωρεῖν κ.τ.λ. listed by Bonitz, we find that a paragraph or a thought is sometimes called φυσικῶς by Aristotle in order to mark some very general difference between this thought and the preceding ones, although it concerns the same topic. The preceding thoughts are sometimes contrasted as λογικῶς or καθόλου, though not in our chapter. We find also, I admit, that Aristotle sometimes seems to be suggesting that the φυσικῶς thought is a better thought and provides a point of view from which the topic appears more distinctly. But I do not find that φυσικῶς thought is *always* better than λογικῶς thought according to Aristotle. I find rather that he meant that φυσικῶς thought is better when one is dealing with physics, and that he sometimes wished to reproach certain philosophers for having treated physics rather as philosophers than as physicists, a criticism which his own eminence as a physicist gave him the right to make. I do not find him thinking that φυσικῶς thought is also the best in inquiries other than physical. It seems probable to me that Aristotle would have held that, just as it can be dangerous to trust to λογικῶς thinking in physics, so it can be dangerous to trust to φυσικῶς thinking in logic.

In our chapter the first three solutions are λογικῶς, though Aristotle does not say so. They give us no information about nature (though the third has much appearance of doing so).

Instead of this, they offer us logical distinctions, between having and using, between the two premisses, and finally between two levels of having. And that is what counts in this matter. To explain how a man can do what he knows to be wrong, although knowledge is powerful or even omnipotent, we need, not facts about human nature, but a logical division of the senses of the word 'know'.

Aristotle adds a φυσικῶς explanation, not in order to get down at last to the question, but rather to satisfy those unfortunate persons who cannot distinguish philosophy from psychology. If you ask me, he says in effect, for information about the acratic's state of mind, I will give you some: the acratic often has in mind a kind of logos, a syllogism of sorts, not indeed the one he ought to have, but another one, favourable to his act. Though Aristotle does not say so, I think I hear him adding under his breath: 'But this pretty psychological story has nothing to do with our question, the answer to which still resides in the logical distinctions I have drawn between the different kinds of knowing.' We note that a little later he refers us to 'the physiologers', if we wish to know 'how the ignorance is dissipated and the acratic resumes his knowledge' (1147b6–9). That is physics, not ethics.

I pass to the third objection. We have been told in Book III, chapter 1, that an act is involuntary, ἄκων, if the agent does not know all the particulars of his act. Let us take the case of Oedipus. Aristotle seems to be telling us here that Oedipus killed his father ἄκων, in that he did not know that the man he killed was his father. The objector infers from this that on my interpretation the acratic act is involuntary, because the absence of the minor premiss is the absence of the knowledge of a necessary particular. But an involuntary act is innocent, whereas the acratic act is blameworthy. A contradiction! The objector proposes to remove the contradiction by denying my view that Aristotle maintains throughout that in acrasia the important syllogism is not fully present.

I reply as follows. Oedipus's ignorance about the man he killed was not the ignorance of a moment or merely of the last degree. Oedipus did not, as soon as the man was dead, come to his senses and exclaim: 'I have killed my father'. It was not until many years afterwards that he learned for the first time that the man was his father. Thus his parricide was genuinely involuntary. He had never known the important fact. The acratic, on the contrary, knows the important fact perfectly well before he commits his act, and he will know it again as soon as the act is done and the desire assuaged. He *has* this essential knowledge, in the technical sense that Aristotle gives to ἔχειν, throughout the duration of his act, and before it, and after it. He also *uses* it, χρῆται, before and after his act. During his act he does not use it. He is blameworthy nevertheless, because he *has* the knowledge all the time.

I pass to the fourth objection, the last objection against my view that I shall mention. This is drawn from the words which Bywater gives us as follows: οὐ γὰρ τῆς κυρίως ἐπιστήμης εἶναι δοκούσης παρούσης γίνεται τὸ πάθος, οὐδ' αὕτη περιέλκεται διὰ τὸ πάθος, ἀλλὰ τῆς αἰσθητικῆς (1147b15–17). Bywater mentions no other importantly different reading. Τῆς αἰσθητικῆς what? Τῆς αἰσθητικῆς [ἐπιστήμης], undoubtedly, although this phrase never occurs and virtually contradicts Aristotle's epistemology. Also without doubt, this 'aesthetic' or perceptual knowledge is what the minor premiss gives us. The sentence opposes this perceptual knowledge to some other knowledge which is κυρίως. Apparently we must conclude that κυρίως knowledge is what is given in the major premiss, that is to say, the moral principle which the acratic disobeys. It follows that the first part of the sentence tells us that 'the passion', that is the acratic act, does not occur in the presence of the major premiss. Hence it occurs only when the major is absent. Hence it is the absence of the *major* premiss which explains acrasia and makes it possible, not the absence of the *minor* as my interpretation maintains.

I reply that the reasoning is correct; but I conclude, not that on account of this one strange sentence we should abandon the view we have collected in reading the whole of the rest of the chapter, but that the text of these strange lines is corrupt and requires emendation. There are two further reasons for thinking that this text is corrupt. (1) The words δοκούσης παρούσης have a suspicious sound. (2) The sentence as it stands contradicts itself. We have seen that its first part means that acrasia is caused by the absence of the major premiss. But its second part denies this. Οὐδ' αὕτη περιέλκεται διὰ τὸ πάθος. That is, the major premiss is not dragged about by the passion. That is, acrasia does not cause absence of the major premiss. It cannot achieve that. It can only render the minor premiss inactive. The major, which is the real knowledge, remains unmoved during the acratic act.

How are we to emend? I know nothing better than Stewart's περιγίνεται: οὐ γὰρ τῆς κυρίως ἐπιστήμης εἶναι δοκούσης περιγίνεται τὸ πάθος. 'The passion does not overcome what seems to be the real knowledge; it is not this which is dragged about by the passion but the perceptual knowledge.' With this emendation the sentence no longer conflicts with my interpretation but confirms it.

CRITICISM OF ARISTOTLE ON ACRASIA

It has been objected to Aristotle that his account of acrasia tells us nothing about the moral struggle, the struggle that a man wages sometimes against a desire and for a moral principle. This is true. But it was not the intention of Aristotle to do so. What he wished to do here was to analyse how one can act contrary to one's principles, whether this act occurs after a struggle or not. He notices elsewhere that such a struggle is possible (1102b17).

A second objection is that this account explains only one of the two forms of acrasia. Aristotle says later (1150b19 ff.)

that there are two sorts of acratic men, the impetuous, who are carried away by the passion because they have not deliberated, and the weak, who deliberate but, owing to the passion, do not abide by the result of their deliberation. My teacher, Sir David Ross, has written that Aristotle's account of acrasia explains at best only the acrasia of impetuous men, not also that of weak men. I take him to imply that, whereas according to Aristotle one commits an acratic act only when some part of the relevant practical syllogism is not completely actual in the mind, in weak acrasia everything is perfectly actual because the man has deliberated.

I think that this objection fails. The weak acratic has indeed deliberated about everything; but it does not follow that the passion cannot still drive out of his mind the premiss which was in it for a time. Aristotle's view is, I think, as follows. The weak acratic deliberates and actualizes the whole of the practical syllogism. But his passion, when it becomes strong, drives some part of the syllogism out of his mind for a moment; and during that moment the acratic commits his act. As to the impetuous acratic, since he never has deliberated, the question how he can do an act that he knows to be wrong does not arise in his case. He has never known that the act is wrong, because he has never realized the minor premiss, because he has not reflected. He is acratic nevertheless, provided that he knows the major premiss, the moral principle, that ought to have operated here.

A third objection, also to be found in Sir David Ross's book (*Aristotle*, London, 1923, p. 224), is that the cause of acrasia lies not in lack of knowledge but in weakness of will. It is held sometimes that the Greeks could not explain acrasia because they lacked the concept of the will. In rejecting this objection, I make use of an idea drawn from Gilbert Ryle's *The Concept of Mind*, namely that weakness of will is not the cause but the form of acrasia. Acrasia is not the effect of weakness of will; it is one of the kinds of weakness of will. To say that acrasia is a weakness of will is to explain it neither more nor less than one explains a crow by saying that it is a bird. Such an explanation is certainly worth giving; but this does not entail that the sort of explanation given by Aristotle is either false or superfluous or even inferior. The same thing admits of several kinds of explanation.

A fourth objection seems better founded. It is necessary to criticize questions beginning with the word 'How?' or 'Πῶς;'. Πῶς ὑπολαμβάνων ὀρθῶς ἀκρατεύεταί τις (1145b21)? 'How does a man with the right view act acratically?' The question 'How?' is perfectly proper in practice. 'How can I get to Lyons?—By taking a train or a plane, sir.' 'How do you do that conjuring trick, sir?—Excuse me, madam; it is a secret.' These 'Hows?' are perfectly correct. They are requests to be told the means which someone uses to achieve a certain end. But in intellectual inquiries, for example when one asks how a man can act contrary to the right, it is a different matter. Here we are not supposing that the acratic possesses some wonderful secret which we want to extract from him. We are not supposing that the acratic has at his disposal some superior means of doing wrong. We are simply supposing that the acratic cannot do wrong. 'How can he?' is a way of saying 'He cannot'.

I suggest that this expression is ill conceived, and that it is a somewhat insincere way of maintaining that acrasia cannot occur. If someone asks you how a man can do what he knows to be wrong, I suggest that you had better reply as follows: 'Experience shows clearly that it is possible to do what one knows to be wrong; so why do you suppose that it is impossible?' By this manœuvre you will make it clear that it is not you but he who ought to give an explanation. For it is he and not you who has asserted a thesis that contradicts experience. Therefore it is he who ought to justify himself. He ought to give you some reason to believe his paradox. If he does not, there is no reason in the world why you should accept it. But he does not. On the contrary, by disguising his thesis as a question beginning with 'How can?', he succeeds in making you think that it is you who are the debtor and the unreasonable man.

Had Aristotle any reason to believe the paradox that a man cannot do what he knows to be wrong? Yes: he believed, like Socrates, that knowledge is stronger than anything else in the mind of a man. 'When knowledge is present, thought Socrates, it is an awful thing that anything else should master it and drag it about like a slave' (1145b23). Like Socrates, Aristotle believed that knowledge is always commanding. Socrates concluded that acrasia does not occur. Aristotle tries to show that acrasia can nevertheless occur, not without raising certain suspicions. But this is too troublesome a way of attaining the end. The simple and good way is to deny the thesis that knowledge is always commanding. It is evident in our experience that it is not always so. If we do this, we no longer need any question beginning with 'How can?'. We need this kind of question only when we deny some fact of experience.

Perhaps you will agree with what I have just said and still demand some explanation of acrasia. For perhaps you will say that it is not enough to submit to experience and recognize the fact of acrasia; we must also understand this strange and repellent fact; we must see something of its place in the totality of human nature. You are right. We must do so; and it will probably be an endless task. For the present, however, I offer you only one thought, a thought which, if true, must help us a little to understand acrasia. It is the thought that moral principles are not discoveries but resolutions. When we adopt a moral principle, we are not deciding how the world is made, but how we are going to act. The principle that one ought not to kill, for example, does not reveal the composition of the world, nor the orders of a god. It takes a stand with regard to the world. The adoption of it constitutes a sort of generalized choice.

If this is so, it follows that when a man acts acratically he acts not contrary to a known fact, so to speak, but contrary to a decision he has taken. Acrasia is not like going through a wall by means of a door which one knows does not exist. It is more like visiting Cologne after having decided not to visit Germany.

These considerations make acrasia more intelligible by putting it into that huge class of contradictions, hesitations, vacillations, incoherences, and absurdities of every kind, which composes a large part of our practical life. Acrasia seemed more mysterious than it is to Aristotle because he assimilated morality to science, in that he regarded the principles of morality as statements of fact, which it would be as impossible to disregard as to disregard a wall that barred our path.

CRITICISM OF ARISTOTLE ON ACOLASIA

Who is this acolastic man of whom Aristotle speaks in the Seventh Book? I doubt whether such a person exists. He is not the acolastic of whom Aristotle spoke in the Second and Third Books. In those books acolasia was not contrasted with acrasia, for Aristotle did not mention acrasia; it was opposed to temperance, and consisted in pursuing a certain kind of pleasure excessively because one was led on by desire. The acolastic had no principle or logos; he was simply led on by desire. And Aristotle did not say whether he afterwards regretted his actions.

In Book VII, on the contrary, the acolastic is contrasted with the acratic rather than with the temperate man; and he appears as a man of principle. He possesses a logos; he obeys his logos; and he does not regret having obeyed his logos.

What is the logos of the acolastic? It can hardly be the logos that 'I ought to pursue excessive pleasures'. For if he used the word 'excessive' he would be condemning himself; and I think Aristotle would have recognized this. But if he condemned himself he would be acratic and not acolastic. It is the acratic who condemns himself. The acolastic has a clear conscience about himself.

We find in the text the principle that 'everything sweet should be tasted' (1147a29). Is this one of the acolastic's principles? If it were, the acolastic would certainly be a mythical person; for there has never been anybody who adopted the principle that everything sweet should be tasted. But I think that Aristotle is not here intending to tell us one of the acolastic's principles. I think rather that he is giving us one of those inappropriate and even absurd examples which unfortunately are not rare in his work.

We read also that the acratic is not persuaded 'that he ought to pursue such pleasures unrestrainedly' (1151a23). Are we to understand that the acolastic, on the contrary, adopts precisely the principle 'that he ought to pursue such pleasures unrestrainedly'? The answer, I believe, is more or less yes.

But to answer the question what principle Aristotle attributes to his acolastic the safest passage is 1146b22, where he expressly says that the acolastic 'is led on intentionally, holding that one ought always to pursue the present pleasure'.

This principle is a bad one according to Aristotle. For the badness of the acolastic consists in his principle's being bad. It does not consist in his disobeying his principle; for on the contrary he obeys it.

Does Aristotle think that the acolastic himself considers his principle bad? He does not explicitly answer this question. But I think he would answer no. For it seems that, if the acolastic himself considered his principle bad, he would thereby too much resemble the acratic, though in a strange and obscure way. So it is only Aristotle who considers the principle bad. The acolastic considers it good.

And which of them is right, the acolastic or Aristotle? If we insist on the 'always', it is evidently Aristotle who is right. There is, unfortunately, no practical principle that one can always follow without ever being in the wrong. But, just because this is too obvious, we ought to doubt whether an acolastic of this sort ever occurs. If, on the contrary, in order to avoid making the acolastic into a man of straw, we do not emphasize the 'always', it becomes much less certain that it is Aristotle who is right. It seems to me that there are fewer men who on principle seek the present pleasure too much than there are men who on principle seek the present pleasure too little. Against puritanism we need to insist that 'we ought to pursue the present pleasure'. This is a duty deriving necessarily from our great duty to alleviate human misery. The duty to restrain our appetite, which of course is often incumbent on us too, also derives from some moral rule justified by the same end, that is, the diminution of human misery.

Aristotle does not discuss the principle with the acolastic. He does not discuss practical principles at all. He hardly even expresses them. I venture to say that this is the greatest defect in his ethics, which nevertheless are magnificent. He did not grasp the fact of moral relativity, the fact, I mean, that sometimes two men, though equally serious and conscientious and obedient to their consciences, nevertheless find their consciences uttering opposed principles. Owing to this fact, we ought to debate moral principles, to discuss them, to defend them, and not to reject other people's principles as evidently false because they do not harmonize with ours. Once we have realized that, among the men who act in ways we disapprove, there are some who do so not because they have no conscience, nor because they flout their own conscience, but because they obey their own conscience and their conscience tells them to act so—once we have realized that, what are we to do? We must not use disapproving words like 'acolastic'. Nor must we use the medical metaphor, as Aristotle too often does, and regard these men as patients to be cured, and even to be cured against their will. The man whose moral principles conflict with mine is to be neither cured nor insulted, but persuaded. I must reason with him and try to convince him; and I must always admit the possibility that in the end it will be I, and not he, who ought to change.

But Aristotle denies the possibility of a rational discussion of the principles of morality. He declares that there is no logos to teach the principles: οὔτε δὴ ἐκεῖ ὁ λόγος διδασκαλικὸς τῶν ἀρχῶν οὔτε ἐνταῦθα, where ἐνταῦθα refers to practice (1151a18). He recognizes only nature and habituation as teachers of morality. That seems to me a great despair. If one day Aristotle happened to think that perhaps he himself had been ill endowed by nature, or ill trained by his teachers, what could he do to reassure himself, either by confirming his principles or by exchanging them for better ones? According to his own theory he could do nothing at all. He says that the bad man does not know he is bad (1150b36); what if one day he overheard this 'bad' man saying to a friend: 'Aristotle does not know that he is bad'?

I believe that we ought to confess our moral principles, and try to make them probable (not to prove them; one cannot prove practical principles), and seek also the reasons against them, and listen to and weigh the principles and reasons of others. By this method we may hope to be always purifying our principles and making them more serviceable for their end, which is the diminution of human misery. It is more or less the same method of approximation as we also follow in the pursuit of the truth about nature. If we adopt this method we continually progress a little towards the end. If we adopt the method of Aristotle we never progress at all, so that, unless we have had the extraordinary luck to be established right on the end by our teachers, we shall never get any nearer to it.